Revolutionary
Kingdom

Revolutionary Kingdom
Following the Rebel Jesus

Revolutionary Kingdom
978-1-5018-8726-0
978-1-5018-8727-7 eBook

Revolutionary Kingdom DVD
978-1-5018-8744-4

Revolutionary Kingdom Leader Guide
978-1-5018-8728-4
978-1-5018-8729-1 eBook

Also from Mike Slaughter

A Different Kind of Christmas

Change the World

Christmas Is Not Your Birthday

Dare to Dream

Down to Earth

Hijacked

Made for a Miracle

Momentum for Life

Money Matters

Real Followers

Renegade Gospel

shiny gods

Spiritual Entrepreneurs

The Christian Wallet

The Passionate Church

UnLearning Church

*Upside Living in a
Downside Economy*

For more information, visit www.MikeSlaughter.com.

Mike Slaughter

with Karen Perry Smith

REVOLUTIONARY KINGDOM

Following the Rebel Jesus

Abingdon Press / Nashville

Revolutionary Kingdom
Following the Rebel Jesus

No part of this work may be reproduced or transmitted in any form or by any means, electronic or mechanical, including photocopying and recording, or by any information storage or retrieval system, except as may be expressly permitted by the 1976 Copyright Act or in writing from the publisher. Requests for permission can be addressed to Permissions, The United Methodist Publishing House, 2222 Rosa L. Parks Blvd., Nashville, TN 37228-1306 or emailed to permissions@umpublishing.org.

Library of Congress Cataloging-in-Publication data has been requested.

978-1-5018-8726-0

19 20 21 22 23 24 25 26 27 28 — 10 9 8 7 6 5 4 3 2 1
MANUFACTURED IN THE UNITED STATES OF AMERICA

Dedicated to our new granddaughter,
Tessa Jillian Slaughter

CONTENTS

INTRODUCTION

In 2013, our Ginghamsburg Church executive leadership team traveled to the North Carolina mountains for a three-day retreat to wrestle with one question: What is a disciple?

We Christians frequently toss the word *disciple* around in our churches, casually using it as both a verb and a noun, while never pausing to examine its powerful implications. If the church's mission is to make disciples of Jesus Christ for the transformation of the world, how will we know when we have accomplished it?

Our team wrestled with this seemingly straightforward question for three days. What emerged after hours of taping scrawled-on sheets of flipchart paper to our meeting space wall was a threefold definition:

1. **The first attribute marking a disciple is an undiluted devotion to Jesus Christ.** For far too long, the Western church has venerated Jesus without making the costly commitment to follow him. The journey to the cross has been traded for a theology of easy "believe-ism," and we have succumbed to the temptation to remake Jesus in our own image instead of being transformed into his. My earlier book *Renegade Gospel: The Rebel Jesus* explores the full implications of making a commitment to Christ.

2. **A disciple of the Rebel Jesus also embraces a kingdom-of-God worldview.** Many of us talk about "Jesus" but view

the world and the people in it through a cultural lens that prioritizes partisan preference, national allegiance, ethnic identity, or economic privilege over Jesus' gospel. This book, *Revolutionary Kingdom: Following the Rebel Jesus*, will require each of us to take a new, serious look at our current worldview lens and realign it with a kingdom-of-God worldview. Some of its pages may make you angry. You may disagree with me on multiple points. That's OK. Let's continue to let Jesus' kingdom-of-God worldview challenge our own cherished assumptions.

3. **The final attribute of a disciple of Christ is practicing a missional lifestyle.** Both *Renegade Gospel* and *Revolutionary Kingdom* include examples of how we are called to practically and faithfully live out the call of Jesus on our lives for the sake of the world God so loves.

The first half of this book will help us unpack the biblical theology of Jesus' kingdom-of-God worldview. The second half will step on our toes as we explore Kingdom politics, economics, and people that may not align with our dearly held perspectives and attitudes.

Revolutionary Kingdom will challenge all Jesus-followers to step out of our places of comfort as we step up, proactively and courageously, to address the economic inequalities and unjust policies afflicting the least, lost, and underserved.

Ready to get a little uncomfortable? Let's get started.

Chapter 1
The Gospel of the Kingdom of God

[Jesus said,] "Now is the time! Here comes God's kingdom!
Change your hearts and lives, and trust this good news!"
Mark 1:15

My initial encounter with Jesus during my late teen years was deeply personal. Raised in the church, baptized as an infant, and confirmed in the sixth grade, my understanding of the Christian faith up to that point had been strictly historical. I knew nothing about a personal encounter with the risen, living Christ.

The Jesus movement of the late sixties and early seventies was in full swing. I immersed myself in a Campus Christian Fellowship group at the University of Cincinnati. We met in dorm rooms and student apartments learning about living life together in communities like the one described in Acts 2. Our community's practices paralleled those of the rabbi Jesus' first-century followers: "The believers devoted themselves to the apostles' teaching, to the community, to their shared meals, and to their prayers" (Acts 2:42). We understood the gospel mandate of the Kingdom meant being heavenly minded, and it necessitated working for earthly good. We participated in planning the first Earth Day (April 22, 1970) to demonstrate support for environmental protection.

Viewing the Vietnam War from a gospel perspective and working together aggressively for civil rights went hand in hand with Bible study and prayer. As Jesus' followers, we saw ourselves representing an alternative politic, the politic of God's kingdom that supersedes all the politics of all the world's kingdoms. We could not separate witnessing and handing out gospel pamphlets from bringing good news to the poor and setting captives free (see Luke 4:18). Jesus gave me a new vision for the teenagers in my hometown community. I taught the very principles and practices I was learning in my college discipleship group to a racially diverse group of high school students back home. "Pass it on" was and is the mantra of discipleship.

Through almost five decades of ministry, I have observed the heresy of privatized faith corrupt Jesus' gospel of the kingdom of God. As I wrote in the first book in this series, *Renegade Gospel*: "When we privatize our faith, we cease to be salt and light in the world. No longer part of a countercultural revolution, or an outpost of heaven demonstrating God's plan for restoration and resurrection, we reduce our faith to this: "Jesus came, died, and rose from the grave to get me into heaven." No! We don't pray to get into heaven; we actively pray and work to get the kingdom of heaven into earth."[1]

A large number of Christians today have confused the gospel of the Kingdom with the politics of the nation-state and have embraced worldly political leaders as ultimate heralds of truth. One influential Christian, Jerry Falwell Jr., who leads the largest Christian university in the US, when asked recently. "Is there anything President Trump could do that would endanger . . . support from you?" answered, "No."[2] The word of God reminds us to restrain ourselves from idolizing worldly leaders:

> *Don't trust leaders;*
>   *don't trust and human beings—*
>   *there's no saving help with them!*
> *Their breath leaves them,*
>   *then they go back to the ground.*
> *On that very same day, their plans die too.*
>   *(Psalm 146:3-4)*

Jesus' first-century followers lived in prophetic tension with the politics of state. The Book of Acts describes how some of the early church's opponents in Thessalonica turned the church's faithfulness to God into a political accusation: "These people who have been disturbing the peace throughout the empire have also come here.... Every one of them does what is contrary to Caesar's decrees by naming someone else as king: Jesus" (Acts 17:6-7).

Jesus' gospel is the good news about the arrival of God's earthly reign. The four Gospels mention this gospel of the "kingdom of God" or "kingdom of heaven" (the phrases are interchangeable) 126 times.

JESUS' GOSPEL OF THE KINGDOM OF GOD

> *Jesus called the Twelve together and he gave them power and authority over all demons and to heal sicknesses. He sent them out to proclaim God's kingdom and to heal the sick.*
>
> *(Luke 9:1-2)*

Jesus framed his understanding of the gospel of "the kingdom of God" within the context of ancient Jewish messianic expectation.

Centuries before Jesus' earthly mission, many in the Jewish community had looked forward to the time when God's reign would be established on earth through a coming messiah. The prophet Zechariah, for example, shared this expectation:

> *Rejoice and be glad, Daughter Zion,*
> *because I am about to come and will dwell among you,*
> *says the LORD.*
> *Many nations will be joined to the LORD on that day.*
> *They will become my people,*
> *and I will dwell among you*
> *so you will know that the LORD of heavenly forces sent*
> *me to you.*
>
> *(Zechariah 2:10-11)*

For some Christians, the hope is not for heaven but rather a time when God returns to reign on earth. Psalm 96 reads,

> *Let the heavens rejoice, let the earth be glad;*
> *let the sea resound, and all that is in it.*
> *Let the fields be jubilant, and everything in them;*
> *let all the trees of the forest sing for joy.*

> *Let all creation rejoice before the LORD, for he comes,*
> *he comes to judge the earth.*
> *He will judge the world in righteousness*
> *and the peoples in his faithfulness.*
>
> (Psalm 96:11-13 NIV)

For many ancient Israelites, judgment had a positive connotation. It meant God was going to bring justice for the oppressed. God was going to set the captive free and lift up the downtrodden.[3]

The world's neglected poor will be first and its self-focused oppressors will be last. Polluted waters will be made fresh. Encroaching deserts will blossom into flowering forests. The psalmist and other ancient Israelites believed the Messiah would come not to take people to heaven but to establish heaven's rule on earth.

The Messiah's coming would mark the beginning of the full restoration of God's created order. In Revelation, the author describes the fullness of creation's restoration at the end of this age:

> *"Look! God's dwelling is here with humankind. He will dwell*
> *with them, and they will be his peoples. God himself will*
> *be with them as their God. He will wipe away every tear*
> *from their eyes. Death will be no more. There will be no*
> *mourning, crying, or pain anymore, for the former things*
> *have passed away." Then the one seated on the throne said,*
> *"Look! I'm making all things new."*
>
> (Revelation 21:3-5)

Eden will be fully restored including the healing of the wounded planet. Water will be made clean and the earth will bear abundant fruit (22:1-2).

Jesus taught his disciples to pray, "your kingdom come, / your will be done, / on earth as it is in heaven" (Matthew 6:10 NIV). When we pray the Lord's Prayer, we are affirming the invasion of heaven's revolutionary rule has begun through Jesus' life, death, and resurrection. Easter is more than remembering that Jesus was raised from the dead. Easter celebrates what Jesus' resurrection has begun: the transformation of all creation.

Christians sometimes believe God will eventually destroy the earth at the end of this age. Absolutely not! Genesis makes clear "God saw everything he had made: it was supremely good" (Genesis 1:31). God's judgment is not to destroy but to fully redeem and restore all of creation. At the end of this age, the world and all it contains will be "firmly in place" (1 Chronicles 16:30).

God revealed through ancient Israel's prophets that a messiah King would come from Judah, one of Israel's twelve tribes (Isaiah 11:1-5). Isaiah paints a picture of the Kingdom's ultimate fulfillment:

> *The wolf will live with the lamb,*
> *and the leopard will lie down with the young goat;*
> *the calf and the young lion will feed together,*
> *and a little child will lead them.*
> *The cow and the bear will graze.*
> *Their young will lie down together,*
> *and a lion will eat straw like an ox.*
> *A nursing child will play over the snake's hole;*
> *toddlers will reach over the serpent's den.*
> *They won't harm or destroy anywhere on my holy*
> *mountain.*
> *The earth will be filled with the knowledge of the* Lord*,*
> *just as the water covers the sea.*

> *On that day, the root of Jesse will stand as a signal to the peoples. The nations will seek him out, and his dwelling will be glorious.*
>
> *(Isaiah 11:6-10)*

Louis Evely had this insightful word:

> To believe in God is to believe in the salvation of the world. The paradox of our time is that those who believe in God do not believe in the salvation of the world, and those who believe in the future of the world do not believe in God.
>
> Christians believe in the "end of the world," they expect final catastrophe, the punishment of others. Atheists in their turn invent doctrines of salvation, try to give meaning to life, work, the future of humankind, and refuse to believe in God because Christians believe in him and take no interest in the world. All ignore the true God: he who has so loved the world!

But which is the more culpable of ignorance?
To love God is to love the world. To love God passionately
is to love the world passionately. To hope in God is to hope
for the salvation of the world.[4]

Jesus boldly proclaimed his fulfillment of the messianic expectation when he read from the scroll of the prophet Isaiah in the synagogue in Nazareth:

> The Spirit of the Lord is upon me,
> because the Lord has anointed me.
> He has sent me to preach good news to the poor,
> to proclaim release to the prisoners
> and recovery of sight to the blind,
> to liberate the oppressed,
> and to proclaim the year of the Lord's favor.
> *(Luke 4:18-19)*

Jesus was, in effect, saying, "The Kingdom revolution of God's redemptive work has established a beachhead on planet Earth, and I am the long-awaited anointed rebel leader of heaven's movement."

When some Pharisees asked Jesus when the kingdom of God would come, Jesus replied, "God's kingdom isn't coming with signs that are easily noticed. Nor will people say, 'Look, here it is!' or 'There it is!' Don't you see? God's kingdom is already among you." (Luke 17:20-21). The kingdom of God is both present now and to come in the future. Heaven's redemptive movement began on the very first Christmas. We look forward to the day of the Lord's return when all of heaven's order will be restored.

A PERSONAL AND SOCIAL GOSPEL

The gospel of the Kingdom has two dynamics. It is both personal and social. John Wesley, founder of the Methodist movement, reminded the church it is impossible to have personal holiness apart from social holiness, or social holiness apart from personal holiness.

Jesus' gospel makes no pretense of dying and going to a disembodied heaven somewhere beyond creation's galaxies. Jesus announced the holistic restoration of heaven's reign on earth. He saw his mission in the context of the Old Testament prophets' social justice demands and the fulfillment of messianic prophecies. The prophet Amos decries institutional worship over God's demand for justice:

> *I hate, I reject your festivals;*
> *I don't enjoy your joyous assemblies.*
> *If you bring me your entirely burned offerings and gifts*
> *of food—*
> *I won't be pleased.*
> *I won't even look at your offerings of well-fed animals.*
> *Take away the noise of your songs;*
> *I won't listen to the melody of your harps.*
> *But let justice roll down like waters*
> *and righteousness like an ever-flowing stream.*
> *(Amos 5:21-24)*

Kingdom justice is not up for partisan political debate. All who become part of Jesus' movement will be working together in community to change oppressive systems that fail to honor the least and the lost. The word of God is definitive:

> *Because you crush the weak,*
> *and because you tax their grain,*
> *you have built houses of carved stone,*
> *but you won't live in them;*
> *you have planted pleasant vineyards,*
> *but you won't drink their wine.*
> *(Amos 5:11)*

There has been a growing disparity between the rich and the poor and a loss of the middle class in the US. This widening gap impacts education, health care, housing and employment opportunities. (We will explore wealth gap more in chapter 5, "Kingdom Economy.")

In a column in *The New York Times*, David Brooks wrote: "Housing and construction rules that keep the poor and less educated away from places with good schools and good job opportunities . . . have a devastating effect on economic growth nationwide."[5] How should we, as followers of Jesus, address this widening gulf between the haves and the have-nots? We cannot cop out by claiming Jesus was only concerned with saving souls and not changing unjust social structures. Followers of Jesus must address issues of economic inequality and unjust political policies.

God holds both individuals and nations accountable for upholding justice for all persons. Take a moment to consider what God has directed through the Holy Scripture:

> *When immigrants live in your land, you must not cheat them. Any immigrant who lives with you must be treated as if they were one of your citizens. You must love them as yourself, because you were immigrants in the land of Egypt; I am the LORD your God.*
>
> *(Leviticus 19:33-34)*

> *"Cursed is anyone who obstructs the legal rights of immigrants, orphans, or widows."*
>
> *(Deuteronomy 27:19)*

> *[God] has told you, human one, what is good and*
> *what the LORD requires from you:*
> *to do justice, embrace faithful love, and walk humbly*
> *with your God.*
>
> *(Micah 6:8)*

> *Hear this, you who trample on the needy and destroy*
> *the poor of the land, saying,*
> *"When will the new moon*
> *be over that we may sell grain,*
> *and the Sabbath*
> *so that we may offer wheat for sale,*
> *make the ephah smaller, enlarge the shekel,*
> *and deceive with false balances,*
> *in order to buy the needy for silver*
> *and the helpless for sandals,*
> *and sell garbage as grain?"*
>
> *(Amos 8:4-6)*

> *Learn to do good.*
> *Seek justice:*
> *help the oppressed;*
> *defend the orphan;*

plead for the widow.
        (Isaiah 1:17)

The LORD of heavenly forces proclaims:

Make just and faithful decisions; show kindness and
compassion to each other!
        (Zechariah 7:9)

Pursue righteousness so that you may live long and take
possession of the land that the LORD your God is giving you.
        (Deuteronomy 16:20)

The righteous know the rights of the poor,
  but the wicked don't understand.
        (Proverbs 29:7)

Texts like these formed Jesus' understanding of his Kingdom mission of social redemption.

Isaiah's prophecies address the misconceptions God's people have when they divorce personal spirituality from social responsibility. Eighth-century Hebrews made the same mistakes many fans of Jesus make today. (Yes, I said "fans" of Jesus, not followers. Jesus said, "Follow me" eighty-seven times in the four Gospels. He said, "Worship me" only twice. We need more followers of Jesus and fewer fans!)

"Why do we fast and you don't see;
  why afflict ourselves and you don't notice?"
Yet on your fast day you do whatever you want,
  and oppress all your workers.
        (Isaiah 58:3)

As followers of the Rebel Jesus, we must work for just minimum wages and health care for all people. Why? Because God has made it clear these are Kingdom priorities. Minimum wage increases have not kept up with higher wage income growth or inflation in the US. A worker paid the federal minimum wage in 2017 could only earn $15,080 working full time.[6] Jesus has given his people the mandate to promote health and healing for all people: "he gave them power and authority over all demons and to heal sicknesses...to proclaim God's kingdom and to heal the sick" (Luke 9:1-2). Demonic powers are the resistant systems, structures, and principalities that stand in the way of God's restorative order.

God's people cannot practice personal, spiritual acts of piety apart from social engagement. Through the prophet Isaiah, God criticized exactly that kind of divide and called the people to a life that integrated personal spirituality and social justice:

> *Is this the kind of fast I choose,*
> *a day of self-affliction,*
> *of bending one's head like a reed*
> *and of lying down in mourning clothing and ashes?*
> *Is this what you call a fast,*
> *a day acceptable to the* LORD?
>
> *Isn't this the fast I choose:*
> *releasing wicked restraints, untying the ropes of a yoke,*
> *setting free the mistreated,*
> *and breaking every yoke?*
> *Isn't it sharing your bread with the hungry*
> *and bringing the homeless poor into your house,*
> *covering the naked when you see them,*
> *and not hiding from your own family?...*
> *If you open your heart to the hungry,*
> *and provide abundantly for those who are afflicted,*
> *your light will shine in the darkness,*
> *and your gloom will be like the noon.*
>
> *(Isaiah 58:5-7, 10)*

THE STATE OF THE CHURCH

I am currently serving in my forty-seventh year of active ministry. I served forty-five of those years in local churches. At the end of 2017, I turned leadership of Ginghamsburg Church, where I had served for more than thirty-eight years, over to other people so I could devote my full time to working with the next generation of church leaders. Since I no longer have the responsibility of leading worship on a weekly basis, I am discovering I have to be very intentional in maintaining the discipline of weekly corporate worship. I'm experiencing firsthand why so many church people disengage from current expressions of the institutional church.

I'm also battling my own cynicism about the church at the same time, and that's not helping me any. We who are the US church can be so unlike Jesus. We so often parrot the divisive pundits who plague our country's partisan politics, and we do it more passionately than we demonstrate the radical politics of God's kingdom, alternative politics that tear down the barriers that divide us. We continue to water down Jesus' radical call to follow him in obedience and self-abandonment. We attempt to domesticate and contain the Holy Spirit in an institutional box we call "church"—a box Jesus has never allowed to contain him.

The institutional church is not the kingdom of God, and neither are we who are its members. But we *are* called to be agents of the Kingdom we can so easily fail to represent.

Let me tell you about one example of how the church can still be agents of the Kingdom.

My daughter and son-in-law used to live in a racially and socio-economically diverse Boston neighborhood. A United Methodist church down the block from their home had, like many in urban areas, experienced several decades of decline. Its congregation of fewer than fifty elderly folks were trying to keep the lights on. A nonprofit organization rented the church basement for $1,000 a month for the purpose of running a 7-day-per-week, 365-days-a-year soup kitchen. They used the room next to the well-worn fellowship hall to distribute clothes. Various volunteer groups brought in food to serve the eighty to one hundred brothers and sisters living in poverty who showed up each evening.

On one night when I visited that church, a young adult group from a nearby Roman Catholic congregation brought and served the food. Now, I don't know how you best connect to Jesus and the reality of his resurrection presence, but I seem to see him best when I hang with those Jesus called "the least of these brothers and sisters of mine" (Matthew 25:40). Hanging out in the humid, 142-year-old basement of a congregation mostly unaware of the mission happening there (apart from the monthly rent payment) gave me the experience of breaking bread with some really special people. Some were struggling in the death grip of addiction; others contended with the paralysis of mental illness. I sat with day workers who would stand in a parking lot waiting for anyone to come and offer them odd jobs. I sat with these precious people and wondered what could happen in our dying congregations if the handful of people sitting in the sanctuary on Sunday mornings would move downstairs the other six days of the week. What can happen when fans commit themselves to becoming followers? What can happen if we dare not just to believe in Jesus, but to *follow* him?

Monika Hellwig was a Roman Catholic theologian at Georgetown University. Her words remind us God's Spirit cannot be tamed: "In my journey...as a Catholic scholar, what have I really learned? First of all, that we cannot keep the Holy Spirit out of the church, no matter how much we try to domesticate the whole enterprise. Second, that the church is wiser and more faithful when it listens discerningly to many voices, even those from outside its own boundaries."[7]

True conversion brings a commitment of social responsibility to work toward closing the divide between the rich and the poor. When the crushing crowds, energized by Jesus' cousin John's message, came out to be baptized, John reminded them what true repentance really means: "Produce fruit that shows you have changed your hearts and lives. . . . Whoever has two shirts must share with the one who has none, and whoever has food must do the same." To the tax collectors who came to be baptized, John said; "Collect no more than you are authorized to collect." To the soldiers who came with the crowd; "Don't cheat or harass anyone, and be content with your pay" (Luke 3:8, 11, 13-14).

Jesus' encounter with the wealthy tax collector Zacchaeus, who he met in Jericho, gives us better insight into the restorative justice understanding first-century followers knew went with conversion. In the assembly of other sinners dining with Jesus, Zacchaeus stood up from the table and said: "Look, Lord, I give half of my possessions to the poor. And if I have cheated anyone, I repay them four times as much" (Luke 19:8). Jesus' response gives us a clearer understanding of the holistic meaning of salvation: "Today salvation has come to this household because he too is a son of Abraham. The Human One came to seek and save the lost" (Luke 19:9-10).

Jesus' mission statement that he read from Isaiah's scroll in his hometown synagogue made the restoration of justice a Kingdom priority:

> The Spirit of the Lord is upon me,
> because the Lord has anointed me.
> He has sent me to preach good news to the poor,
> to proclaim release to the prisoners
> and recovery of sight to the blind,
> to liberate the oppressed,
> and to proclaim the year of the Lord's favor.
> *(Luke 4:18-19)*

My sisters and brothers, if the gospel is not good news for the poor it is not the gospel of Jesus!

> *He has sent me . . .*
> *to bind up the brokenhearted,*
> *to proclaim release for the captives,*
> *and liberation for prisoners,*
> *to proclaim the year of the* LORD's *favor*
> *and a day of vindication for our God,*
> *to comfort all who mourn,*
> *to provide for Zion's mourners,*
> *to give them a crown in place of ashes,*
> *oil of joy in place of mourning,*
> *a mantle of praise in place of discouragement.*
> *(Isaiah 61:1-3)*

This is what the gospel of Jesus we say "yes" to in answering his call to follow him is like. We will become fully committed to join his community to

> *rebuild the ancient ruins,*
> *[to] restore formerly deserted places;*
> *[to] renew ruined cities,*
> *places deserted in generations past.*
> *(Isaiah 61:4)*

Why? For "I, the LORD, love justice: / I hate robbery and dishonesty" (v. 8).

Jesus' long discourse concerning the final day of judgment

amplifies this Kingdom mandate. He tells his disciples about his coming return with the angels of heaven:

> *"Then the king will say to those on his right, 'Come, you who will receive good things from my Father. Inherit the kingdom that was prepared for you before the world began. I was hungry and you gave me food to eat. I was thirsty and you gave me a drink. I was a stranger and you welcomed me. I was naked and you gave me clothes to wear. I was sick and you took care of me. I was in prison and you visited me.'....*
>
> *"'I assure you that when you have done it for one of the least of these brothers and sisters of mine, you have done it for me.'"*

(Matthew 25:34-36, 40)

Clarence Jordan, who earned a doctorate in New Testament studies from Southern Baptist Seminary in Louisville, founded Koinonia Farm near Americus, Georgia, in 1942. He designed the farm as an experiment in communal Christian living. He saw racial reconciliation between blacks and whites as the rural South's greatest need—a view considered dangerously radical at the time in the community where he ministered. After the Supreme Court's decision in *Brown v. Board of Education* (1954) began school desegregation, Koinonia was subjected to violent terrorist attacks and an economic boycott. Jordan believed "the problems with Christianity stemmed from the fact that most Christians pictured Jesus enthroned in heaven or safely confined to 'Bible Times,' thus missing the challenge of the incarnation." By glorifying Christ, he wrote, "We more effectively rid ourselves of him than did those who crucified him." He also stated, "Faith is not belief in spite of evidence but a life in scorn of the consequences."[8]

Some of you at this point might be feeling the pinch of political undertones. The gospel of the Kingdom demands Christian engagement in the political systems of the world. We must hold the political principalities and powers accountable for ensuring full justice and working for the well-being of all God's children. Albert Mohler, the president of Southern Seminary and Boyce College, said, "I truly believe that we're called to be involved in every arena of life, but never simply on the terms set by any given human endeavor....So, Christians will, of necessity, if faithful, be politically engaged. But that doesn't always mean that we operate with a political strategy or that we are understood to have any hope of being on the winning side. We have a greater requirement for faithfulness."[9]

Our political involvement must never compromise the gospel's revolutionary demands by being identified with a worldly partisan political party. Jesus' statement that his Kingdom was not of this world (John 18:36) did not mean it was distant and otherworldly. Jesus' kingdom stands in prophetic tension with all political partisan platforms, conservative or progressive, as well as the self-serving religious institutions. Why was he crucified? He was considered an enemy by both during his time on earth.

Now here is the hard part in this equation. Jesus warned those who would dare follow him:

> *"If the world hates you, know that it hated me first. If you*
> *belonged to the world, the world would love you as its own.*
> *However, I have chosen you out of the world, and you*
> *don't belong to the world. This is why the world hates you.*
> *Remember what I told you, 'Servants aren't greater than*
> *their master.' If the world harassed me, it will harass you too."*
> *(John 15:18-20)*

Archbishop Oscar Romero of San Salvador spoke boldly against the oppressive government regime stealing farmland from the poor and silencing protesters through murder. Romero openly criticized the US government for backing the military junta that seized control of the national government in 1979. While celebrating mass on March 24, 1980, in the chapel of the Hospital of Divine Providence, he was assassinated at the altar, at the age of sixty-two.[10]

Romero reminds us the church cannot stand silent in the face of social injustice. "A church that does not provoke crisis, a gospel that does not disturb, a word of God that does not rankle, a word of God that does not touch the concrete sin of the society in which it is being proclaimed—what kind of gospel is that?"[11]

Romero defined the great need for today's church:

The great need today is for Christians who are active and critical, who don't accept situations without analyzing them inwardly and deeply. We no longer want masses of people like those who have been trifled with for so long. We want persons like fruitful fig trees, who can say yes to justice and no to injustice and can make use of the precious gift of life, despite of the circumstances.[12]

Misplaced Allegiance—The Flag or the Cross?

We are experiencing a growing tide of nationalism and with it a spirit of isolationism throughout our world. In our own country, a nationalistic zeal is promoting the attitude of "country first, country forever." Our borders start to become sacrosanct and "outsiders" become suspicious, something to be feared. The Syrian conflict that began in March 2011 has created one of the worst humanitarian crises in recent times. More than 13 million people in the country need humanitarian assistance, and more than 5.6 million Syrians have fled the country as refugees. Another 6.2 million people are displaced within Syria.[13] European countries have made moves to close borders and make immigration more restrictive. In June 2016, Britain voted to leave the European Union. Debate about building walls and making immigration much more restrictive dominated the 2016 US presidential election.

As of this writing, a caravan of thousands of Central American migrants is trekking through Mexico. It is made up of weary families seeking asylum in the United States. I am not so naïve as to believe there are not folks in this group who have criminal intentions. But I also know there are families seeking asylum for protection from the drug cartels threatening the lives of their children.

What does the Bible have to say about our response to these human needs? What does it mean to face these tough issues with a kingdom-of-God worldview? Why does nationalism contradict God's restorative Kingdom movement?

Jesus' disciples were guilty of making the same assumption many Christians through the centuries have made. Even after his miraculous resurrection, they dared to ask him, "Lord, are you going to restore the kingdom to Israel now?" (Acts 1:6) They were still looking for a political savior who would "make Israel great again." Jesus' response made it clear God's new covenant movement no longer favored a particular people or individual nation. "It isn't for you to know the times or seasons that the Father has set by his own authority. Rather you will receive power when the Holy Spirit has come upon you, and you will be my witnesses in Jerusalem, in all Judea and Samaria, and to the end of the earth" (Acts 1:7-8).

To the end of the earth! Yes, the Kingdom movement is about including all nations and all peoples. For God so loves the world! An early Christian creed, recited when believers were being baptized, affirmed this truth of radical inclusion: "There is neither Jew nor Greek; there is neither slave nor free; nor is there male and female, for you are all one in Christ Jesus" (Galatians 3:28).

Yes, God did choose Israel as a special people. They were not chosen, however, for privilege, but for God's divine purpose. "Since the whole earth belongs to me[, you] will be a kingdom of priests for me and a holy nation" (Exodus 19:5-6). God had promised Abraham, "All the earth's nations will be blessed because of [you]" (Genesis 18:18).

We must always see Jesus' kingdom-of-God movement in prophetic tension with the empire-of-nation state. The gospel of the Rebel Jesus moves beyond nationalistic favoritism to global redemption.

The cross, not the flag, should be at the center of Christian identity and worship. As followers of the Rebel Jesus, we are a Kingdom people. The earliest Christian creed, "Jesus is Lord," had lethal ramifications for those who accepted Jesus' call to follow in the way of the cross. They refused to acknowledge Caesar as Lord. Yet so many in the church today have subjugated Christian faith to the gods of nationalistic allegiance.

A pastor recently shared an example of how she has had to confront this twisted heresy:

> As a young female pastor in Mississippi, I had to choose carefully where to put my foot down. The folks in my newly appointed congregation said the pledge of allegiance during worship on Sunday mornings. They said the Lord's Prayer,

the pledge of allegiance to the American flag and then the Christian flag, took the offering and sang the doxology. As for the pledges, I just stood silently every time. Every Sunday I moved the American flag a smidge closer to the door, with the intent of eventually getting it out of the sanctuary. After three years, someone noticed. That's when people also noticed I was not practicing the pledges, but just standing through them silently, which culminated in a three-hour-long meeting where they tried to convert me from Jesus-following to Christian nationalism.

They were completely convinced that you cannot separate loyalty to country (and the Republican party to be exact) from loyalty to Jesus.

It befuddles me when I see churches flying the Christian flag under the American flag. What does this say about Jesus' ultimate authority and our ultimate allegiance? Mike Jordan Laskey, former director of Life and Justice Ministries for the Diocese of Camden, addresses our contested loyalties: "Because Christians belong to a community that transcends national boundaries and politics, they should be wary of churches that hold nationalistic celebrations or sing patriotic songs and of church leaders who cozy up to political figures. American flags don't belong in church sanctuaries, where the focus should be on the crucified Christ, whom Christians worship and follow."[14]

The psalmist reminds us to "not put your trust in [political] princes, / in human beings, who cannot save" (Psalm 146:3 NIV). Why? Because we are children of God's kingdom who have but one ultimate allegiance. Jesus is Lord!

So how does the revolutionary kingdom of God differ from nationalism? Nationalism brings people together through pride of feeling and identity. "Our citizenship is in heaven. We look forward to a savior that comes from there—the Lord Jesus Christ" (Philippians 3:20). Followers of Jesus identify as citizens of the revolutionary kingdom of God, committed to following the way of the Rebel Jesus, serving his mission while we await his return. We are to be an alternative society governed by the Spirit of Christ.

CHAPTER 2

THE COUNTERCULTURE KINGDOM COMMUNITY

*You yourselves are being built like living stones into a
spiritual temple. You are being made into a holy priesthood
to offer up spiritual sacrifices that are acceptable to God
through Jesus Christ. . . . You are a chosen race, a royal
priesthood, a holy nation, a people who are God's own
possession. You have become this people so that you may
speak of the wonderful acts of the one who called you out of
darkness into his amazing light.*

(*1 Peter 2:5, 9*)

Three faiths—Judaism, Christianity, and Islam—claim Abraham
as their patriarchal ancestor. God calls Abraham, at the youthful
age of seventy-five, to leave all that was familiar to him and establish
a beachhead community for God's kingdom movement, in a
land strategically connecting three continents. God's mission for
Abraham begins locally with diverse tribes of Semitic people but
will ultimately expand to all the earth:

*I will make of you a great nation and will bless you. I will
make your name respected, and you will be a blessing.*

*I will bless those who bless you,
those who curse you I will curse;
all families of the earth
will be blessed because of you."*

(*Genesis 12:2-3*)

God enters into a covenant relationship with communities of people called out of the general population to carry out God's redemptive mission on earth. A covenant is an agreement between two parties who commit to keep promises to and carry out responsibilities for each other. The word for "church" in New Testament Greek is *ekklesia*, which means "called out ones." These communities become colonies of heaven on earth, visible expressions of God's kingdom.

Moses' calling to lead God's people comes almost five centuries after Abraham's. The Kingdom movement that began with God's promise to Abraham will now be passed to a nomadic group of Semitic desert tribes. God directs Moses to lay out the provisions of God's covenant with people who had lived as slaves, immersed in a polytheistic culture for four hundred years: "This is what you should say to Jacob's household and declare to the Israelites: You saw what I did to the Egyptians, and how I lifted you up on eagles' wings and brought you to me. So now, if you faithfully obey me and stay true to my covenant, you will be my most precious possession out of all the peoples, since the whole earth belongs to me. You will be a kingdom of priest for me and a holy nation" (Exodus 19:3-6). We can't gloss over the fact that God calls former slaves, the least and the weak, and not the world's elite and powerful.

God calls Israel to become a countercultural group of missionary priests. The people's lifestyles and moral, ethical values will stand in stark contrast to the ways of the surrounding nations and communities. This chosen people will radiate light in the abyss of the world's darkness. God's choosing of the community of "peculiar people" is always to service, never to privilege.

Jesus models the Kingdom's countercultural ethic in his response to the mother of two of his disciples, who asked for special privilege for her sons. His reply must have felt like a stinging rebuke: "You don't know what you're asking!" Jesus then asks a question we must each answer for ourselves. "Can you drink from the cup that I'm about to drink from?" (See Matthew 20: 20-22.) The call of Jesus is always the call to sacrifice.

He continues the conversation with laserlike focus on the alternative way for the community of God's kingdom: "You know that those who rule the Gentiles show off their authority over them and their high-ranking officials order them around. But that's not the way it will be with you. Whoever wants to be great among you will be your servant. Whoever wants to be first among you will be your slave—just as the Human One didn't come to be served but rather to serve and to give his life to liberate many people" (Matthew 20:25-28). Take a moment to stop here and reflect. Ask yourself, "Am I willing to make myself available in any way, great or small, to serve God's will?"

The Narrow Way

The revolutionary kingdom requires a new way of thinking and a new way of life most are unwilling to adopt. Many who begin the journey never finish. John's Gospel reminds us, "Many of his [Jesus'] disciples turned away and no longer accompanied him" (John 6:66). Why? "Many of his disciples . . . said, 'This message is harsh. Who can hear it?'" (verse 60). If our faith journey is not challenging us in significant ways, then we are traveling on the wrong path!

Isaiah wrote about a future path of life that would be opened: "A highway will be there. / It will be called the Holy Way. / The unclean won't travel on it, / but it will be for those walking on that way. / Even fools won't get lost on it" (Isaiah 35:8). Jesus claimed to be that "Way" (John 14:6), and he reminded his followers to "Go in through the narrow gate. The gate that leads to destruction is broad and the road wide, so many people enter through it. But the gate that leads to life is narrow and the road difficult, so few people find it" (Matthew 7:13-14). The way of obedience and losing one's life to discover true life will never be popular in our contemporary culture, obsessed as it is with the self.

Robert Frost's poem, "The Road Not Taken," has always reminded me of the decision every true disciple of Jesus must continually make in the commitment to follow him.

Two roads diverged in a yellow wood,
And sorry I could not travel both

And be one traveler, long I stood
And looked down one as far as I could
To where it bent in the undergrowth;

Then took the other, as just as fair,
And having perhaps the better claim,
Because it was grassy and wanted wear;
Though as for that the passing there
Had worn them really about the same,

And both that morning equally lay
In leaves no step had trodden black.
Oh, I kept the first for another day!
Yet knowing how way leads on to way,
I doubted if I should ever come back.

I shall be telling this with a sigh
Somewhere ages and ages hence:
Two roads diverged in a wood, and I—
I took the one less traveled by,
And that has made all the difference.

Jesus calls us to follow him in his countercultural way of life. Remember, eighty-seven times in the four Gospels Jesus says, "Follow me," and only twice, "Worship me." Following Jesus means we will be going where Jesus is going, doing what Jesus is doing, and being who Jesus is being. Kingdom people embody divine mercy and grace for the purpose of demonstrating God's grace and mercy in the communities in which they live and work.

Jesus became the visible model for our missional lifestyles. "I assure you that whoever believes in me will do the works that I do. They will do even greater works than these because I am going to the Father" (John 14:12). Take a moment to reflect on this promise. God's miraculous works will be done through our hands! This countercultural community, empowered through the Holy Spirit's supernatural gifts and graces, literally becomes the body of Christ on earth. We become Jesus' hands and feet, exponentially replicating his works throughout the world. Through the indwelling Holy Spirit, we are naturally supernatural!

On the first Pentecost after Jesus' ascension, God sent the Holy Spirit to Jesus' followers, fulfilling these words from the ancient prophecy of Joel:

> In the last days, God says,
> I will pour out my Spirit on all people.
> > Your sons and daughters will prophesy.
> > Your young men will see visions.
> > Your elders will dream dreams.
> Even upon my servants, men and women,
> > I will pour out my Spirit in those days,
> > and they will prophesy.
> > > *(Acts 2:17-18)*

God creates each of us with a purpose. Every one of us is given different gifts of the Spirit for the purpose of contributing to God's redemptive mission on earth.

> *There are different spiritual gifts but the same Spirit; and there are different ministries and the same Lord; and there are different activities but the same God who produces all of them in everyone. A demonstration of the Spirit is given to each person for the common good.*
> > *(1 Corinthians 12:4-7)*

Please note the gifts of the Spirit are never given for self-promotion or recognition, but for the well-being of all. God's mission depends on each and every one of us functioning in our life calling and unique mix of gifts. "You are the body of Christ and parts of each other" (1 Corinthians 12:27).

I have written about Ron Will's story before, but I feel it's important to give an update on his visionary ministry's miraculous growth. Ron and his wife, Mary Jo, have served Christ's mission faithfully as small group leaders, as marriage coaches, and through various mission endeavors as members of Ginghamsburg Church. Ron has spent the majority of his career as a lead software project contractor at Wright Patterson Air Force Base in Dayton, Ohio. Ron calls this his day job. He discovered his real life calling at age sixty-two. He shared with me how it happened. He was sitting in worship on a particular Sunday morning when the preacher's message was about life calling. "God spoke to me just as clearly as you and I are sharing together right now, Mike. Through that inner voice, I heard God say, 'Ron, what are you going to do with the rest of your life?'"

Ron had some exposure to the growing epidemic of drug and alcohol addiction throughout Dayton and the surrounding communities. He personally knew families who had been devastated by the loss of employment and, eventually, death. That's when Ron heard God's prophetic voice to get up and go.

Joshua Recovery Ministries is the miraculous result of Ron's obedience. This nonprofit ministry started small in 2008, with one residential house for men who needed help recovering from drug and alcohol addiction. The mission statement on the ministry's website defines its purpose as setting people free from drug and alcohol addiction. "We accomplish this through Christlike care, and sharing Christian principles that help the person value one's self, loved ones, and community. We believe all addictions are sicknesses that require a person to look to God, personal counseling, and encouragement of others on the road to their recovery."[1] In ten years' time, the program has grown to include six men's residential houses and a counseling center. It is currently preparing to open two homes for pregnant women in addiction's grip.

For its first several years, Ron led this ministry while being fully employed in his day job. He is now retired and able to pursue his "burning bush" calling from God full time. And I might add, Ron has never taken a dime for doing this work! As a follower of the Rebel Jesus, Ron has fully embraced his Lord's mandate: "You didn't choose me, but I chose you and appointed you so that you could go and produce fruit and so that your fruit could last. As a result, whatever you ask the Father in my name, he will give you. I give you these commandments so that you can love each other" (John 15:16-17).

THE WAY OF LOVE

It's a disturbing trend seen across America: the percentage of millennials raised in a church who are now abandoning their faith is growing. According to a 2014 Barna research study:

- Only 2 in 10 Americans under 30 believe attending a church is important or worthwhile.
- 59 percent of millennials raised in a church have dropped out.
- 35 percent of millennials have an anti-church stance, believing the church does more harm than good.[2]

You don't have to spend much time surfing the web to get a picture of how outsiders perceive the church. One source states, "A full 72 percent of the people interviewed said they think the church is full of hypocrites."[3] Go ahead and search the internet for yourself. You will find, "selfish, not really interested in others," "self-centered, judgmental and anti-gay"—the list of negative perceptions seems endless.

The twentieth-century pacifist Indian Hindu leader, Mahatma Gandhi (1869–1948) struck at the core of the real problem when he stated, "I like your Christ; I do not like your Christians. Your Christians are so unlike your Christ." Embodying the kingdom of God's DNA makes it necessary for us to align our minds and hearts with God's character and will.

Witnessing Jesus' transfiguration, three of his disciples experienced one of those mountaintop spiritual highs (Mark 9) that folks often have after attending a weekend retreat. Some of you have been there and done that, and if you have, you also know the reality of coming back down the "mountain" to the weekly routines of daily living.

The Gospel of Mark goes on to tell us that when Jesus and the three disciples came down from the mountain to rejoin the others, "they saw a large crowd surrounding them and the legal experts arguing with them" (Mark 9:14). The legal experts were defenders of orthodoxy, committed to keeping all 613 commandments found in the Pentateuch (the first five books of the Old Testament).

At this point, Jesus asked his disciples a very pertinent question: "What are you arguing about" (Mark 9:16)? Such a relevant question for the church today! A cutting question for a church whose arguments so often reflect the bitter political and religious divides occurring across the globe. Arguing has brought my own

United Methodist tribe to the brink of schism, even though the vast majority of us agree on the basic orthodox tenets of trinitarian faith. No wonder so many people outside the church can't see Jesus in the anti-Christ behavior of those of us who profess his name but betray his character. Jesus challenged those who readily said "yes" to his invitation without calculating the cost of following: "Not everybody who says to me, 'Lord, Lord,' will get into the kingdom of heaven. Only those who do the will of my Father who is in heaven will enter" (Matthew 7:21).

God is a God of relationships. God values our relationships' priority and health above our partisan doctrines and political differences. One of the legal experts asked Jesus to name the single most important law from all the commandments. Jesus replied:

> *"The most important one, is* Israel, listen! Our God is the one Lord, and you must love the Lord your God with all your heart, with all your being, with all your mind, and with all your strength. *The second is this:* You will love your neighbor as yourself. No other commandment is greater than these."
>
> *(Mark 12:29-31)*

The teacher of the law heartedly agreed.

There is a subtlety here in Jesus' response we must not overlook. Notice he indicates the two commandments are truly one by changing the plural "commandments" to the singular "commandment." You can't love God if you don't love your neighbor, and you can't really love your neighbor in the same way Christ loves us if you don't love God. "When Jesus saw that he had answered with wisdom, he said to him, 'You aren't far from God's kingdom'" (Mark 12:34).

It has always amazed me that, in everything written about Jesus in the Gospels, we find he gave only one new commandment: "I give you a new commandment: Love each other. Just as I have loved you, so you also must love each other. This is how everyone will know that you are my disciples, when you love each other" (John 13:34-35). That's it! People will recognize Christ when our lives and relationships embody his love. Don't get caught up in partisan camps.

People will not find Jesus in our political alliances, denominational divides, or doctrinal arguments. Love wins!

The countercultural community of God's kingdom will be known because it radically embodies Jesus' sacrificial love:

> *You have heard that it was said,* You must love your neighbor *and hate your enemy. But I say to you, love your enemies and pray for those who harass you, so that you will be acting as children of your Father who is in heaven."*
>
> *(Matthew 5:43-45)*

Jesus demonstrated the ultimate weapon of spiritual warfare; love ALL others as God loves you. *All* means All! And yes, *all* also includes our enemies!

Let me give you a personal example.

On Father's Day 2007, I woke up in an NGO (nongovernmental organization) compound in Ed Daein, Darfur, that was surrounded by nine-foot walls topped with embedded broken glass and barbed wire. My son, 25 years old at the time, lay in a cot covered with mosquito netting just a few feet away. In less than an hour we would be undertaking a risky, three-hour journey into the rebel-held territory of Adilla in East Darfur.

In Adilla, we met with Muslim leaders in a clay brick structure that housed the local official's offices. Ginghamsburg's outreach had been working in this area through the building of schools and sustainable water yards for over two years, along with our partner, the United Methodist Committee on Relief (UMCOR). The leaders thanked us and assured us we could continue our work unharmed because we were bringing much needed resources to their people. One Muslim Sheikh even asked me why we Christians were helping Muslim people. That was the first opportunity, after two years of productive work in the area, that opened the door for me to tell about Jesus who came to tear down the walls that divide all people."[4]

Jesus explained love as the alternative weapon of warfare:

"You have heard that it was said, An eye for an eye, and a tooth for a tooth. But I say to you that you must not oppose those who want to hurt you. If people slap you on your right cheek, you must turn the left cheek to them as well. When they wish to haul you to court and take your shirt, let them have your coat too. When they force you to go one mile, go with them two."

(Matthew 5:38-41)

Jesus' hard-core directive was not just a theoretical proposition. If a Roman soldier stopped a Jewish person and asked for their coat, under Roman law that person had to give it up. This mandate was a military strategy Rome used to outfit its armies during the winter months. The strategy enabled Roman forces to move far beyond traditional supply points into further territories of conquest. And if a Roman soldier asked a Palestinian Jew to carry his pack, by Roman law that person, living under the oppression of an occupying enemy, was required to carry the soldier's supplies one mile, but no more. The soldier would then choose another bystander to carry his load for the next mile. Jesus' directive demonstrated the radical, "take the enemy by surprise" alternative to the world's weapons of violence, oppression, power, and control.

Writer Amy Kuebelbeck has some great insight concerning a Christian response to evil:

> Jesus goes even further. He says not to resist one who is evil. But he doesn't say not to resist evil itself. He doesn't say to shrug and look the other way when harm is being inflicted on others. What Jesus offers is another way to resist evil, such as being more generous than required. Perhaps our response to evil could be so countercultural and so unexpected that a persecutor would be bewildered and thrown off balance—sort of like jiu jitsu, the art of unarmed self-defense that leverages one's own weakness to counter another's strength.[5]

As Archbishop Romero demonstrated, Jesus' call to his church is costly. If the gospel we are teaching and practicing isn't unsettling to some people, it probably isn't the gospel.[6] The church is called out to fight heaven's battles. But we must not fight heaven's battles with hell's weapons! "Our weapons that we fight with aren't human, but instead they are powered by God for the destruction of fortresses" (2 Corinthians 10:4).

As Jesus' followers, we must not let ourselves be lured into the politics of hate by the fear of our enemies. We must realize the fiercest defense against evil is ultimately the proactive demonstration of Christ's love. The people of God's kingdom are meant to be the visible demonstration of heaven's redemptive purpose on earth. Through this community of faith, God is creating a Kingdom culture markedly different from the political alliances of earthly kingdoms. Jesus' selection of the original twelve apostles appeared an unlikely group for the cohesive start of a Kingdom movement. It was truly a unifying work of the Holy Spirit that brought to fruition the missional work of unity in the midst of such diverse political persuasions.

Matthew was a tax collector in the employ of the oppressive Roman political system when Jesus called him to follow. By aligning with Rome, tax collectors were helping the Empire exploit their fellow Jews. Simon the Zealot represented the opposite extreme of the political spectrum. The Zealots viewed the Romans as pagan oppressors occupying God's Promised Land. Along with the Romans came their false gods and unacceptable ways of thinking and living. The Zealots favored armed rebellion against Rome and were not hesitant to resort to terrorist tactics when they deemed such tactics necessary. Jesus' selection of Simon seems strange considering he taught nonviolence. There were probably no two groups of Jews in Palestine who hated each other more than the tax collectors and the Zealots.

And then there's Judas Iscariot. Why did he betray Jesus? We are on shaky ground when we try to guess his motive. But I would dare to go out on a limb and say it wasn't about the blood money he received for his act of treachery. Many people were looking for a political messiah who would "drain the swamp" by defeating the controlling Roman administration and make Israel "great again" by restoring the Davidic kingdom. Judas couldn't accept what appeared to be Jesus' subservience and apparent defeat at the hands of oppressive Roman dominance. Judas made the same mistake many in the church do today. He allowed his political ideology to determine his biblical theology.

As followers of the Rebel Jesus, we represent an alternative party, the party of the kingdom of God. As Jesus' disciples, we must be moving forward in the Spirit of Pentecost, tearing down demeaning barriers that divide and destroy. How can we find our way forward in demonstrating unity without expecting uniformity? I don't know about you, but I don't want to miss out on all God has created. I want to join all my politically, socioeconomically, and ethnically diverse neighbors at the Kingdom's open table! (In chapter 6, we will push ourselves to explore this topic more.)

The work of the cross is God's work of reconciliation. We love God by loving others in spite of our ideological differences. In a world obsessed with building walls to keep people out, followers of the Rebel Jesus are tearing down walls of exclusion and ideologies that separate and divide people from each other.

> *Christ is our peace. He made both Jews and Gentiles into one group. With his body, he broke down the barrier of hatred that divided us . . . so that he could create one new person out of the two groups, making peace. He reconciled them both as one body to God by the cross, which ended the hostility to God.*
>
> *When he came, he announced the good news of peace to you who were far away from God and to those who were near. We both have access to the Father through Christ by the one Spirit.*
>
> *(Ephesians 2:14-18)*

Aliyah Bing is a young African American high school student. As her pastor, I have had the privilege of watching her grow in faith and spiritual maturity. She gifted me with a copy of a paper she wrote describing the unique diversity that reflects the community of God's people:

> We are God's Mosaic. A mosaic is a work of outstanding artistry that produces a picture or pattern produced by

arranging together small colored pieces of material. When you think of the kingdom of God, there is a vast array of people. There are different nations and ethnicities. People of all ages and personalities. People with unique and special qualities that make them intricate human beings. The difference within God's people shows just how great of a creator God is. God chose to take things that were once separated and joined them together into a masterpiece for God's glory.

Aliyah gets it. God's diverse countercultural community, through the indwelling Spirit, becomes the divine gene pool from which the world is being re-created in God's image.

Notice the diversity of nations represented in Jerusalem on the Day of Pentecost (Acts 2:5-11). The Holy Spirit came like a flood to create a new community of people no longer separated by the walls of nation-state, ethnicity, or language:

> All the believers were united and shared everything. They would sell pieces of property and possessions and distribute the proceeds to everyone who needed them. Every day, they met together in the temple and ate in their homes. They shared food with gladness and simplicity. They praised God and demonstrated God's goodness to everyone. The Lord added daily to the community those who were being saved.
> (Acts 2:44-47)

What a community! No wonder the movement was growing so rapidly. Folks were demonstrating an alternative way of being together in community that wasn't based on uniformity. You could agree to disagree and still be included in the family. Look at the people God invite to come, sit down, and feast together in the Kingdom: "Go quickly to the city's streets, the busy ones and the side streets, and bring the poor, crippled, blind, and lame" (Luke 14:21). Jesus was considered a heretic by the keepers of orthodox correctness because of the crowd he unapologetically invited to his dinner.

The apostle Peter had a religious prejudice against non-Jews. God had to break through Peter's elitist theological barrier in order to get him to become who God was calling him to be in the Kingdom movement. In a vision, Peter heard the voice of God: "Never consider unclean what God has made pure" (Acts 10:15). As a result, Peter quickly turned from his convoluted belief: "I really am learning that God doesn't show partiality to one group of people over another. Rather, in every nation, whoever worships him and does what is right is acceptable to him" (Acts 10:34-35).

WHOM ARE YOU LISTENING TO?

Three of Jesus' disciples witnessed an unexplainable event on the mountain of Jesus' transfiguration (Mark 9:2-7). I have to believe their life-altering experience wasn't caused by the psychoactive plants and herbs used for many centuries in religious contexts for mind-altering experiences. Jesus' appearance was "transformed in front of them, and his clothes were amazingly bright. . . . Elijah and Moses appeared and were talking with Jesus" (verses 2, 4). A voice is heard coming from the covering of a cloud, "This is my Son, whom I dearly love. Listen to him!" (verse 7).

Who are you listening to? A recent Pew Research Report found two-thirds of Americans are getting their news from social media. Ready for this? Facebook is the number one source, followed by Twitter, YouTube, and Snapchat.

Over the past thirty years, Americans have seen a substantial shift in the way news is reported. American news sources have moved from informing people about world events in an unbiased way to reporting the news with the goal of influencing our perspectives and votes from biased, partisan political perspectives. People turn to the news source that best supports their political agenda, whether liberal or conservative, and denounce others as "fake news."

As followers of Jesus, we must be careful to guard our hearts and minds against letting others interpret the signs of the times for us. Who are we allowing to shape what we value, how we think and vote, and what we believe? Who are we listening to? God still says, "This is my Son, whom I dearly love. Listen to him!"

HEARING THE WORD OF GOD

Jesus' parables often highlight our ability or inability to hear and see spiritual truths that transcend the confines of cultural ideologies. Jesus told the parable of the sower who scattered his seed in four different types of soil:

> *"Some fell on the path; and the birds came and ate it. Other seed fell on rocky ground where the soil was shallow. They sprouted immediately because the soil wasn't deep. When the sun came up, it scorched the plants; and they dried up because they had no roots. Other seed fell among thorny plants. The thorny plants grew and choked the seeds, and they produced nothing. Other seed fell into good soil and bore fruit. Upon growing and increasing, the seed produced in one case a yield of thirty to one, in another case a yield of sixty to one, and in another case a yield of one hundred to one." He said, "Whoever has ears to listen should pay attention!"*
>
> (Mark 4:4-9)

This parable brings us back again to the importance of receiving our life perspectives and values from heaven's directives. Jesus reminds his disciples to, "Listen carefully!" (Mark 4:24). Why did three out of four soils fail to produce a crop? The problem wasn't with the seed. The quality of the seed (the Word of God) was the same. Kingdom health depends on the receptive quality of the soil in which the seed is sown. "The seed scattered on good soil are those who hear the word and embrace it. They bear fruit, in one case a yield of thirty to one, in another case sixty to one, and in another case one hundred to one" (Mark 4:20).

Hateful rhetoric has become a daily constant. From the highest offices of the American government to the church pew, we hear words that blame, shame, and demonize those with whom we disagree. Racism has been emboldened. Violence in demonstrations and protests is a growing trend. Followers of the Rebel Jesus must not forget his words: "What goes out of the mouth comes from the heart. And that's what contaminates a person in God's sight" (Matthew 15:18). The words we speak are the true test of character.

What do the words that you speak, text, post, or tweet reveal about your heart?

Words have power! "The tongue has the power of life and death" (Proverbs 18:21 NIV). The words that flow from our mouths have the power to create unity or division. Have you ever said or posted something that you wish you hadn't? Words spoken can't be taken back.

A friend recently told me about his family's Thanksgiving Day dinner table "blow up." The family was equally divided about the status of the current head of state as well as the nation's political differences, so you can probably guess what the blow up was all about. An older brother, who had earlier given the Thanksgiving blessing, got up from the table and announced he would never return to his younger sibling's house. The animosity will probably blow over eventually, but even when the words we speak may be forgiven, they are not easily forgotten.

Why were Jesus' disciples arguing with the legal experts? Why do we argue with those with whom we disagree? We argue because we want to convince others we stand on the side of truth. The disciples wanted to let the guardians of the law know, with no uncertainty, Jesus was on their side. They were technically right but relationally wrong. God is a God of relationships, as revealed in the oneness of the Trinity. Jesus prayed for our unity: "I'm not praying only for them [Jesus' disciples] but also for those who believe in me because of their word. I pray they will be one, Father, just as you are in me and I am in you. I pray that they also will be in us, so that the world will believe that you sent me" (John 17:20-21).

Right relationship wins over right argument! John Wesley described God's missional purpose as: "To spread the fire of heavenly love over all the earth" affirming that: "Love is the end, the sole end, of every dispensation of God." [7]

I am convinced we are living in a time of seismic spiritual transition in the church. God is doing a new thing! Old institutional religious systems of governance are passing away. Denominational walls are falling down. Christ will be seen in the midst of a counter-cultural community, emptied of self, living immersed in God's love.

CHAPTER 3
REVOLUTIONARY AUTHORITY

In the past God spoke to our ancestors through the prophets at many times and in various ways, but in these last days he has spoken to us by his Son.

(Hebrews 1:1-2 NIV)

October 31, 2017, marked the five-hundred-year anniversary of the beginning of the Protestant Reformation. Martin Luther, a German theologian, priest, and monk, rediscovered the Scriptures' authority out of his frustration with the compromising, shifting traditions of the institutional church. He strongly protested the Catholic practice of indulgences (paying the church to reduce the penalty of sin). Luther experienced God's voice in a fresh new way while studying the Book of Romans. His emphasis on the primacy of Scripture, "Sola Scriptura," fanned the flames of revolutionary reformation. His radical writings resulted in his excommunication by Pope Leo X in 1521, and his condemnation as an outlaw by the Holy Roman Emperor. Luther translated the Bible into the common language of the masses, which inspired both Protestant and Catholic renewal.

Nearly two hundred years later, John Wesley heard God's voice while attending a Moravian Bible study group. The group was studying Luther's notes on the Book of Romans. Wesley's life, and the lives of millions of others influenced by his teachings, would never again be the same. He became "a man of one book." For Wesley, the Bible was the last word in guiding Christian faith and practice:

> The Christian rule of right and wrong is the Word of God, the writings of the Old and New Testament; all that the prophets and "holy men of old" wrote "as they were moved by the Holy Ghost."[1]
> My ground is the Bible. Yea, I am a Bible-bigot. I follow it in all things, both great and small.[2]

Rutilio Grande (1928–1977) was a Jesuit priest in El Salvador. He entered the Jesuits at age seventeen but later had a second conversion. Through the Scriptures, he found a renewed sense of calling to defend the poor. His work for the rights of the poor caused him to be labeled a radical and an enemy of the oppressive system. On March 12, 1977, the van he was traveling in was sprayed with gunfire, killing him and the two people traveling with him.

Grande understood the radical message found in the Bible that works toward the fulfillment of God's kingdom on earth. "Very soon the Bible won't be allowed to cross our borders," he wrote. "We'll get only the bindings, because all the pages are subversive."[3]

WHO HAS THE RIGHT WORD ON THE WORD?

The Reformation brought the church back to a renewed awareness of the primacy of the Holy Scripture as the authority for faith and practice. But through the five centuries that followed there have been major disagreements in how the Scriptures should be interpreted. Arguments over right interpretation have resulted in continued schisms. My own Methodist family has experienced multiple divisions over issues of biblical interpretation. Look at how many Methodist bodies exist as I write:

- The Wesleyan Church
- The Church of The Nazarene
- The Free Methodist Church
- The Primitive Methodist Church
- The African Methodist Episcopal Church

- The African Methodist Episcopal Zion Church
- The Congregational Methodist Church
- The Evangelical Methodist Church
- The Bible Missionary Church
- The United Methodist Church
- Various Holiness and Pentecostal Branches

All of these churches, as well as the thousands of others in the world, would claim the same Scriptures validate true faith and practice. Our debates concerning women in leadership, immigration, and sexuality, to name but a few issues, are not about biblical authority in and of itself. All of us would generally agree the authority of Scripture is the basis for our faith, lifestyle, and missional calling. Our disagreements are centered in our understanding of biblical interpretation.

For example: People have used the Scriptures listed below, and others like them, to support the institution of slavery, the repression of women, and the use of abusive force to discipline children.

The women should be quiet during the meeting. They are not allowed to talk. Instead, they need to get under control, just as the Law says. If they want to learn something, they should ask their husbands at home. It is disgraceful for a woman to talk during the meeting.

(1 Corinthians 14:34-35)

I want women to enhance their appearance with clothing that is modest and sensible, not with elaborate hairstyles, gold, pearls, or expensive clothes. . . . A wife should learn quietly with complete submission. I don't allow a wife to teach or to control her husband. Instead, she should be a quiet listener.

(1 Timothy 2:9, 11-12)

When a slave owner hits a male or female slave with a rod and . . . the slave gets up after a day or two [before dying], the slave owner shouldn't be punished because the slave is the owner's property.

(Exodus 21:20-21)

*Slaves, obey your human masters with fear and trembling
and with sincere devotion to Christ.*

(Ephesians 6:5)

*Don't withhold instruction from children;
    if you strike them with a rod, they won't die.
Strike them with a rod,
    and you will save their lives from the grave.*

(Proverbs 23:13-14)

Would these Scriptures represent the way of Jesus, who welcomed women disciples? Methodists stood on the floor of the General Conference of 1956 and quoted the Bible to justify not ordaining women, a practice a majority of Christians around the world still follow.

What about slavery? Methodists stood on the floor of the 1844 General Conference and quoted the Bible to defend slavery, then voted to split the church.[4]

We need to deal with critical questions concerning biblical interpretation. How does God's revelation in Jesus change the way we interpret the Bible? What parts of Scripture are descriptive of people's perceptions of God at the time they were written, and so need to be viewed through the lens of their cultural experience? What parts of Scripture are culturally timebound, and what parts are timeless, authoritative for all generations?

I was one of the 864 delegates who met in Saint Louis in February 2019 for the Special Session of The United Methodist General Conference, called to deal with schism within my own tribe. Those tumultuous days are symptomatic of a spiritual cancer infecting the Western church as a whole. Passionate Christians on all sides of many contentious issues—environmental advocacy, LBGTQ inclusion, immigration, and others—advocate vehemently for their own viewpoint or theological interpretation. We can find it much more enticing in the heat of the moment to loudly rail against opposing viewpoints, claiming biblical authority. Wasn't that the Pharisees' grounds of argument against Jesus, even to the point of seeking Jesus' death?

We have failed to demonstrate the unity our rebel leader prayed for:

> *I'm not praying only for them [Jesus' disciples] but also for*
> *those who believe in me because of their word. I pray they*
> *will be one, Father, just as you are in me and I am in you. I*
> *pray that they also will be in us, so that the world will believe*
> *that you sent me. I've given them the glory that you gave me*
> *so that they can be one just as we are one. I'm in them and*
> *you are in me so that they will be made perfectly one.*
> *(John 17:20-23)*

Tony Campolo, a well-known speaker, preacher, author, and activist, is a spellbinding storyteller. Tony's delivery is always powerful. But I would have to say my all-time favorite anecdote of his is the story of a "preach-off" held at Tony's largely African American church in West Philadelphia several years ago. Tony was one of the pastors preaching and ended his turn in the pulpit feeling pretty good about himself and his oratory's effectiveness. As Tony tells it, though, he was soon humbled when his seasoned, elderly black pastor took the platform and out-preached Tony, summing up his message with five words, repeated in a captivating cadence that soon brought the congregation to its feet: "It's Friday, but Sunday's coming."

Right now in the mainline American church, it feels like Friday. Recent blogs have declared the death of Christianity in America and speculated Jesus has left his church. I sometimes find myself in agreement. How can outsiders ever experience the depth of Jesus' love when those of us who claim it fail to demonstrate Jesus' revolutionary love to each other? To the unchurched we appear to be irrelevant at best and vehemently exclusive and fear-mongering at worst.

In John's Gospel, we read about religious leaders who want to execute a woman based on a literal interpretation of Old Testament Law.

> *The legal experts and Pharisees brought a woman caught*
> *in adultery. Placing her in the center of the group, they*

> *said to Jesus, "Teacher, this woman was caught in the act*
> *of committing adultery. In the Law, Moses commanded*
> *us to stone women like this. What do you say?" They said*
> *this to test him, because they wanted a reason to bring an*
> *accusation against him.*
>
> *(John 8:3-6)*

In other words, Jesus, "What is your doctrinal stance on this issue based on the Word of God?"

The religious leaders' litmus test of truth was centered in the literal interpretation of Scripture that mandated the execution of women, which had been carried out for centuries and still is in some areas of the world.

> *If the claim [of adultery] is true and proof of the young*
> *woman's virginity can't be produced, then the city's elders*
> *will bring the young woman to the door of her father's*
> *house. The citizens of that city must stone her until she dies*
> *because she acted so sinfully in Israel by having extramarital*
> *sex while still in her father's house.*
>
> *Remove such evil from your community!*
> *(Deuteronomy 22:20-21)*

There are many other Old Testament texts that call for the execution of both men and women for violating God's Law. Biblical execution could be carried out for dishonoring your father by being promiscuous (Leviticus 21:9); being a witch (Exodus 22:18); being an enemy of Israel (Hosea 13:16); incest (Leviticus 20:12); bestiality (Leviticus 20:16); being psychic (Leviticus 20:27); raping an engaged woman (Deuteronomy 22:25); getting raped and not screaming loud enough (Deuteronomy 22:23-24); or not being a virgin on your wedding night, a law that applied only to women (Deuteronomy 22:13-22). Having sex while menstruating would require the exile of both the man and woman, which would culminate in their death in the desert where they lacked both food and water (Leviticus 20:18).

Jesus shed new light on scriptural interpretation. "Whoever hasn't sinned should throw the first stone." The men began to drop their rocks and walk away. "Woman, where are they? Is there no one to condemn you?" She answered, "No one, sir." Jesus quickly replied, "Neither do I condemn you. Go, and from now on, don't sin anymore" (John 8:7-11). God is Lord of life, not a god of wrath who wills vengeful death and destruction. Jesus is the living Word of God, revealing the infinite love and patience of an eternal Father.

Yet how often are we guilty of insisting on our own rigid interpretations of Scripture to the great harm of others? How do we Christians assassinate each other by throwing figurative stones at each other in defense of our particular interpretation of Scripture? In one of his sermons, Pope Francis said, "The hardest stone that exists in the world: the tongue."[5]

Agreeing to Disagree

The same Spirit who led the Protestant Reformers was also moving among those committed to staying in the Roman Catholic Church. A clear focus on Christ as the focus of faith and daily practice was at the heart of the Counter-Reformation, also called the Catholic Revival. As A. G. Dickens writes; "And even after Luther's revolt, the highest Catholic achievements were those of men and women who believed themselves to be seeking Christ rather than fighting Luther."[6]

Ignatius of Loyola (1491–1556) was to the Catholic Church and Counter-Reformation what Luther was to the Protestant Reformation. Loyola had a conversion experience six years after Luther's, but was committed to renewal within the Catholic Church. He founded the Society of Jesus (the Jesuits) with the express purpose of renewing the church and taking Christ to the unchurched people of the world.

Teresa of Avila (1515–1582) and St. John of the Cross (1542–1591) were reformers who also played key roles in the renewal of the Catholic Church. Both had a consuming passion to experience and make known Christ, the Living Word of God. They taught the church much about the necessity of personal time spent with Christ in prayer and meditation.

Yes, God can use the unrest that comes from our disagreements to bring much-needed renewal. American author Phyllis Tickle has written in her book, *The Great Emergence: How Christianity Is Changing and Why*, that Christianity undergoes revolution every five hundred years. Every five hundred years a paradigm shift turns the institutional order upside down and replaces it with a fresh wind from the Spirit. The Reformation was one of those revolutions.

I had the privilege of working with Phyllis several years ago on a film project. She shared with me over dinner and a craft beer that she believed Christianity was currently in the middle of a revolutionary shift that would birth Kingdom renewal. My question to Phyllis and other influential leaders is, "How do we agree to disagree over biblical interpretation and maintain the unity in the Spirit Christ prayed for?" As the apostle Paul wrote to the Church at Ephesus, "Make an effort to preserve the unity of the Spirit with the peace that ties you together. You are one body and one spirit, just as God also called you in one hope. There is one Lord, one faith, one baptism, and one God and Father of all, who is over all, through all, and in all" (Ephesians 4:3-6).

There is a richness in Catholic practice expressed in the church's ability to live in paradox—the tension of both-and. It's what theologian Karl Barth referred to as, "that damned Catholic 'and'"; both Scripture and tradition, both faith and works.

I recently spent a couple of days in Assisi, Italy, studying the mission and ministry of St. Francis (1181–1226). Francis turned his back on his family's wealth and became a Catholic friar. He was renowned for his powerful preaching and austere lifestyle based on Christ's passion for the poor. He founded what has become known as the order of the Franciscans.

Francis challenged the church's doctrine on substitutionary atonement. Broadly speaking, this doctrine teaches Jesus' death saves us because he dies in our place—as our substitute—on the cross, paying the price for sin we never could. Francis didn't believe this blood atonement was required for God to love or forgive us. Jesus didn't die to change God's mind about humanity but to change humanity's mind about God. This position marked a radical departure from the orthodox position on the atonement at the time, as well as for the majority of the Western church today. You can understand why folks screamed charges of heresy against Francis!

Pope Innocent III made the judgment that Francis' position on the atonement wasn't heresy but deemed it a minority view within the context of the Christian community. Francis, along with his theology, remained in the Roman Catholic fold.

THE KEY QUESTIONS

What do we mean when we affirm the primacy of Scripture and when we call it authoritative for faith and practice? What in it is absolutely essential? What is open to disagreement or changed interpretation? Several critical insights in the Scriptures can guide us in our journey together.

Let's take a look at Jesus' interaction with a group of religious leaders following his healing of a man at the pool of Bethsaida who was paralyzed. Once again, we find people disagreeing not over the authority of Scripture, but how to interpret its deeper meaning. When the devil tempted Jesus in the wilderness, the devil quoted Scripture correctly but got its meaning wrong (Luke 4:9-11), so we should all take note before jumping too quickly into disagreement about Scripture with others!

We'll join this encounter between Jesus and religious leaders in the fifth chapter of the Gospel of John: "The Jewish leaders were harassing Jesus, since he had done these things on the Sabbath" (verse 16). Our picture of God will always impact our interpretation of Scripture. If we view God as the cosmic judge whose relationship with us is based on rule-keeping, we will judge others on the basis of their adherence to our interpretation of God's rules.

Jesus shifts the paradigm in his response to the religious leaders' indignation: "My Father is still working, and I am working too" (verse 17). We discover in Jesus' response a radical shift from the orthodox position of the day. "For this reason the Jewish leaders wanted even more to kill him—not only because he was doing away with the Sabbath but also because he called God his own Father, thereby making himself equal with God" (verse 18).

God is Father! This Father is all-loving, compassionate, and forgiving. God is the intimate parent who seeks our well-being 24/7. The New Testament community had a picture of God that was very different from those the religious leaders who criticized Jesus had. It was a picture that impacted the earliest Christians' relationships with God and each other. "Dear friends, let's love each other, because love is from God, and everyone who loves is born from God and knows God. The person who doesn't love does not know God, because God is love" (1 John 4:7-8). God is all about relationships. It is of no benefit to be doctrinally correct and relationally wrong!

The followers of the Rebel Jesus also had a new revolutionary authority. Let's get back to Jesus' interaction with those religious leaders at Bethsaida and hear again his bold claim:

> *I have a witness greater than John [the Baptist]'s testimony.*
> *The Father has given me works to do so that I might*
> *complete them. These works I do testify about me that the*
> *Father sent me. And the Father who sent me testifies about*
> *me. You have never even heard his voice or seen his form,*
> *and you don't have his word dwelling with you because*
> *you don't believe the one whom he has sent. Examine the*
> *scriptures, since you think that in them you have eternal life.*
> *They also testify about me, yet you don't want to come to me*
> *so that you can have life.*
>
> *(John 5:36-40)*

Talk about a radical shift in the understanding of ultimate authority! The religious leaders sought absolute truth and authority in the Scriptures. Jesus makes it clear Scripture is neither the source of life nor God's final word. "In the past, God spoke through the prophets to our ancestors in many times and many ways. In these final days, though, he spoke to us through a Son. God made his Son the heir of everything and created the world through him" (Hebrews 1:1-2). God's Word has become flesh and has lived among us. The authority of the Living Word now supersedes the authority of the written word!

We become complacent when we worship the Bible rather than the Living Word through whom all things were made. Our English translations of the Bible put us at a disadvantage when referring to the Word of God. The Greek New Testament uses two different words to distinguish between the written and Living Word. *Grapho* means "write," or "writing." The word is used to describe the Holy Scripture but was also used in reference to other written works. *Logos* means "Word," referring to the living Christ among us and in us. The apostle Paul distinguishes between the written Scripture and that which was received new from the Living Word:

> *We also thank God constantly for this: when you accepted*
> *God's word [Logos] that you heard from us, you welcomed*
> *it for what it truly is. Instead of accepting it as a human*
> *message, you accepted it as God's message [Logos], and it*
> *continues to work in you who are believers.*
>
> *(1 Thessalonians 2:13)*

The Living Word is now working in and speaking through those of us who believe!

So the question becomes, where do we find our authority for faith and practice, and why is there room for us to agree to disagree on the nonessentials?

When Jesus left, he didn't say he would leave us with a book. "I will ask the Father, and he will send another Companion, who will be with you forever. This Companion is the Spirit of Truth, whom the world can't receive because it neither sees him nor recognizes him. You know him, because he lives with you and will be with you. I won't leave you as orphans. I will come to you. Soon the world will no longer see me, but you will see me. Because I live, you will live too. On that day, you will know that I am in my Father, you are in me, and I am in you" (John 14:16-20).

Jesus didn't give us a book of rules defining the parameters of God's will for all ages. Jesus gives us his living presence! "The Companion, the Holy Spirit, whom the Father will send in my name, will teach you everything and will remind you of everything I told you" (John 14:26). So how will the Holy Spirit lead us in navigating twenty-first-century issues first-century believers didn't have to concern themselves with?

Jesus' teachings in the four Gospels were never meant to be final and definitive for all time:

> *"I have much more to say to you, but you can't handle it now. However, when the Spirit of Truth, comes, he will guide you in all the truth. He won't speak on his own, but will say whatever he hears and will proclaim to you what is to come. He will glorify me, because he will take what is mine and proclaim it to you. Everything that the Father has is mine. That's why I said that the Spirit takes what is mine and will proclaim it to you."*
>
> (John 16:12-15)

We see this living, dynamic presence of the Holy Spirit guiding first-century Jesus-followers in situations that called for changing previously held beliefs. In the Book of Acts, we read about a Roman Army officer named Cornelius, a Gentile who is described as God-fearing, who has a concern for the poor and who prays regularly. Through a heavenly vision, Cornelius is moved to send for the apostle Peter. Peter has a vision while praying the next day that will result in a revolutionary shift in what the church would become. In a trance-like state Peter "saw heaven opened up and something like a large linen sheet being lowered to the earth by its four corners. Inside the sheet were all kinds of four-legged animals, reptiles, and wild birds." While still in the contemplative state, Peter hears a voice, "Get up, Peter! Kill and eat!" (Acts 10:11-13).

Even though Peter was a totally committed follower of Jesus, he still kept Jewish dietary laws. Jesus must not have discussed these laws with Peter before his ascension, but Jesus knew Peter would be able to follow the present Holy Spirit's leading when the time came. Peter attempts to remind God what is spiritually unacceptable: "Absolutely not, Lord! I have never eaten anything impure or unclean." Three times a response was repeated to Peter: "Never consider unclean what God has made pure" (verses 14-15).

Peter was then moved to go with the men Cornelius had sent for him. When Peter entered Cornelius's house, he found a large gathering of people. Peter told them, "You all realize that it is forbidden for a Jew to associate or visit with outsiders. However, God has shown me that I should never call a person impure or unclean" (Acts 10:28). The risk Peter took to obey the voice of the Holy Spirit opened the door for the inclusion of all God's children in the Christian church.

Peter stood on a conviction that did not come from a book but through the inner voice of the Holy Spirit:

> *"I really am learning that God doesn't show partiality to*
> *one group of people over another. Rather, in every nation,*
> *whoever worships him and does what is right is acceptable*
> *to him. This is the message of peace he sent to the Israelites*
> *by proclaiming the good news through Jesus Christ: he is*
> *Lord of all!"*
>
> (Acts 10:34-36)

Peter continues to tell the good news of the gospel, resulting in a dramatic Holy Ghost revival (see verses 44-46)!

The Holy Spirit is dynamic, moving, and expanding our understanding of God. God doesn't change (see Hebrews 13:8), but our understanding of God does. Richard Rohr, a Franciscan friar and author, speaks of the evolving, transforming work of the Holy Spirit in our lives and world:

> The New Testament shows history working in a way that is both evolutionary and positive. See, for example, Jesus' many parables of the Kingdom, which lean heavily on the language of growth and development. He uses metaphors of the seed, the maturing ear of corn, weeds and wheat growing together, and yeast rising. His parables of the "Reign of God" are about finding, discovering, being surprised, changing roles and status. None of these notions are static; they are always about something new and good coming into being.[7]

Led by the Holy Spirit, the church has rightly discerned and moved past culturally bound biblical text on many issues. The New Testament church, for example, no longer accepted plural marriage. As another example, consider the fact that my great-great-grandfather was a Mississippi slave owner and quoted biblical text to support that demonic practice. It's hard to believe this sin against humanity was still being carried out almost two thousand years after the New Testament was written!

Renewal is personal, but also spills out into social institutions. Every great awakening has had a resulting major effect on society's moral, economic, political, and cultural foundations. Historian William G. McLoughlin goes so far as to say the great awakenings in American history have influenced most of our nation's social reforms. He contends that they are "the catalysts of social change."[8] As the church is moved through the Holy Spirit, she moves against evil forces that oppress God's people. A renewed church of transformed people fought slavery and illiteracy, and sent armies of missionaries around the world to preach the good news of God's Kingdom movement and break the bonds of poverty and oppression. Wesleyan renewal brought a moral and spiritual strength that averted a potential civil war in England and created many just changes in a corrupt neo-Industrial age. The church was at the heart of the struggle against racism in the 1960s. We need a renewed revolutionary movement today to carry on the continuing battle against the demonic forces of nationalism, isolationism, and fear of other. For God so loves the world!

We must not allow ourselves to be caught in the political spirit of the age. We are citizens and children of the kingdom of God. We always have to look at the written word through the eyes and Spirit of the Living Word. I found a quote from Dorothy Day (1897–1980), who cofounded the Catholic Worker Movement, written in the margin of my Bible. I am not sure of the source, but the quote refers to Paul's statement on slavery (Ephesians 6:5). "Slaves, obey your human masters with fear and trembling and with sincere devotion to Christ." Dorothy Day asks the right question: "Where were the saints to try to change the social order, not just to minister to the slaves but to do away with slavery?"[9]

The people of the Kingdom must always live in prophetic tension with the unjust systems of the world, led and empowered by Christ

Jesus' living presence. Day's quote goes on to state, "By crying out unceasingly for the rights of workers, of the poor, of the destitute . . . we can throw our pebble in the pond and be confident that its ever widening circle will reach around the world."[10]

We must be careful not to fall into the trap of cultural relativity. The question of authority brings us back to the "both-and" I mentioned earlier in this chapter. Our authority is not Scripture itself, but Scripture enlightened by the living presence of the Holy Spirit, and interpreted in the trust and accountability of community.

UNITY IN DIVERSITY

So how can we demonstrate the unity our Lord calls us to live before the world in community when we have significant differences in interpreting Holy Scripture?

Corinth was one of ancient Greece's largest and most important cities. The temple of the Greek god Apollo was the central hub from which the city's acclaim grew. Corinth has been described by a classical scholar as

> the Greek port that is depicted as the free-living "Amsterdam of the ancient world." After landing at the Corinthian docks, sailors would apparently wheeze up the thousand-odd steps to the top of a stunning crag of rock called the Acrocorinth, which offered 360-degree vistas of the sparkling Mediterranean. There they would pass beneath the marble columns of the Temple of Aphrodite, goddess of Beauty and Love, within whose incense-filled, candlelit confines 1,000 comely girls supposedly worked around the clock gathering funds for their deity.[11]

You can imagine the challenges Paul faced in this center of diverse Greek and Roman philosophies and a pantheon of pagan gods. Not only did the church at Corinth face the issues of cultural diversity, but it also had to deal with ethnic and language barriers. How can God's Kingdom people ever demonstrate the alternative Kingdom community in the midst of ideological and cultural differences?

Paul reminds us our unity is based in one absolute. He writes in his first letter to the Corinthians, "I had made up my mind not to think about anything while I was with you except Jesus Christ, and to preach him as him crucified" (1 Corinthians 2:2).

Yes! That is the one absolute. In unity, we follow our revolutionary authority Christ Jesus, the Way, the Truth, and the Life, under the guidance of the Holy Spirit. Our unity is not based on doctrinal correctness, but in our baptism into Christ: "We were all baptized by one Spirit into one body, whether Jew or Greek, or slave or free, and we all were given one Spirit to drink" (1 Corinthians 12:13).

I am serving in my forty-seventh year of active ministry. The issues that have confronted the church in my time—civil rights, immigration, creation care, sexuality—continue to divide God's people. Ginghamsburg Church, where I served for thirty-eight years as lead pastor, welcomes *all* people. I was recently asked by a long-term member about our church's stance in the denomination's LGBTQ debate. My reply, "Our stance is Jesus. Everything else is a conversation!"

Now that we have unpacked Rebel Jesus' view of the kingdom of God, in the next three chapters we will uncover exactly how radically different the revolutionary kingdom is from the cultural worldview and practices many of us who identify as Christians have too readily adopted.

Chapter 4
Kingdom Politics

When I aimlessly scroll through the news feed on my smartphone while waiting at my doctor's office or sitting in a store parking lot waiting for my wife to run into the grocery store, I find my eyes frequently drawn to headlines featuring a number. If you put "The Top Ten Ways to" at the start of the headline, I am almost always compelled to read the rest of the article, no matter what the subject is. It could be about ways to save money on your groceries, improve productivity, or annoy your coworkers. I also love those top five (or ten) lists naming the highest paid actors, most influential books, frequently visited beaches, or chart-topping music singles of the year.

One such list that recently caught my eye was *CEOWorld Magazine*'s 2018 list of the most powerful people in the world. President of the United States Donald Trump was number one, followed by Russian President Vladimir Putin as number two, with Chinese President Xi Jinping finishing out the top three. Then German Chancellor Angela Merkel came in at number four, representing the only woman within the top ten.[1] You may have either high or little regard for one or more of the names on that list, but either way, they are not names that typically leave a person feeling warm and fuzzy on the inside.

Curious to see if this rather subjective list was in agreement with other sources, I turned to *Forbes Magazine*, whose list had been published five months earlier. The top four names were the same as *CEOWorld's*, except Trump and Xi Jinping's positions were flip-flopped.[2] As you moved further down both lists, those who appeared were either politicians holding the highest seat of power within their country or wealthy capitalists with amazing fortunes, often acquired by founding companies that provided products or services that had disrupted and revolutionized one industry or another. The sole exception was Pope Francis, who appeared on one list in the sixth spot and on the other in the eighth spot. Perhaps it's no surprise the top political leaders from both lists were those from countries known to be nuclear powers.

Both publications had selected those who appeared on their lists using identical criteria: how many people they had power or influence over, the financial resources they controlled, if they had power across multiple spheres, and how actively they used their power to change the world—whether for the better or the worse. I found myself speculating as I scrolled through: If these lists based on that criteria had been published circa AD 33 or thereabouts, I deeply doubt Jesus would have made either one.

During my morning devotions on the same day I had viewed the "most powerful" lists, I had spent time in Psalm 136. The psalmist extolls God's many attributes and accomplishments: goodness, superiority over other gods, creative abilities, miracles, power over entire peoples and kings, and provision of daily needs. Yet the only attribute lifted up repeatedly is this: "God's faithful love lasts forever!" This refrain is repeated twenty-six times in a twenty-six-verse psalm. Again with the possible exception of Pope Francis, none of the 2018 top ten most powerful people were known first and foremost for their love. In fact, I could argue a few on the 2018 list wield a power far more about the fear or destruction of others than it is about love eternal.

Power, as described in God's revolutionary kingdom, is counter-cultural. While power in part today is derived from one's access to nuclear missile launch codes, power in the Kingdom is built around relationship. When Adam and Eve, in their pride, disobeyed the one rule the one true God had given them to follow, God didn't blow them up. We soon find God walking in the garden, seeking Eve and Adam out, calling this newly fallen humankind back to himself. Their sin had consequences, and difficult ones, but God never failed—then or now—to exercise love and faithfulness.

Jesus was at the powerful apex of his earthly ministry when he, as the suffering servant, knelt with a towel to wipe his disciples' filthy feet. He soon hung beaten, bruised, and seemingly helpless on his enemies' rough-hewn cross. Important as they were, the heady early days of Jesus' earthly ministry, when he was able to draw a crowd of thousands to hear him preach on a Galilean hillside, did not represent the peak of his power.

Paradoxically, the apostle Paul made it evident our access to God's power is often through acknowledging our own weakness. In 2 Corinthians 12:7, Paul describes being plagued by some painful "thorn in my body." It's not clear exactly what it was, but Paul prayed to be healed of it. Ultimately, however, he acknowledged the pain's redemptive power, declaring, "Therefore, I'm all right with weaknesses, insults, disasters, harassments, and stressful situations for the sake of Christ, because when I'm weak, then I'm strong" (2 Corinthians 12:10). "Weakness" was not even close to being a "most powerful people" selection criterion for *Forbes* or *CEOWorld*. But what the world may consider "foolish" becomes revolutionary and powerful in the light of God's Kingdom purposes.

Perhaps nowhere else is the upside-down "foolishness" of revolutionary kingdom politics more evident than in the Beatitudes, part of that hillside speaking engagement that starts Jesus' Sermon on the Mount in Matthew 5. Let's look at these sayings with fresh eyes, assessing the Kingdom attitudes, the countercultural "be-attitudes," that position us to inherit the kingdom of God.

Blessed Are the Poor in Spirit

When Jesus saw the crowds, he went up on a mountainside and sat down. His disciples came to him, and he began to teach them. . . .

> *"Blessed are the poor in spirit,*
> *for theirs is the kingdom of heaven."*
>
> *(Matthew 5:1-3 NIV)*

To align our lives with Kingdom values, we first need to deal with the root of our brokenness in today's selfie-crazy, social media-driven culture: self-absorption. In my brokenness, it's easy for my point of reference to become me, not Jesus. Everything quickly becomes about my needs, my desires, my happiness. In fact, in this cult of self, "happiness" becomes the ultimate value. We become convinced our meaning is primarily found in the pursuit of happiness. So we surround ourselves with things we believe will make us happy: toys, entertainment, technology, pricey vacations. We paint our lives as picture-perfect on Instagram, and admire politicians, celebrities, and pundits who amass large Twitter followings to demonstrate their power or popularity.

In the Sermon on the Mount, Jesus offers a stark contrast to this self-centered lust for happiness. It's called blessedness. To be blessed runs much deeper than temporal happiness. Happiness is based on our circumstances—if we have good health, a decent job, money, and comfortable relationships, we can be happy. But, change just one of those circumstances, and happiness quickly flies out the door. Being blessed, on the other hand, brings a joy that is not hostage to our life's circumstances. So if health goes, a job is lost, or the fabric of a relationship tears, we still have the assurance of a joy in Jesus no one can take away from us.

When we believe we are in control of creating our own happiness, we quickly fall into the trap of self-reliance. We think, "I can do it. I can handle it. I'm strong. I can stop any time I want to stop. I can climb my way to the top of next year's 'most powerful people' list all by myself." It is not that we stop believing in God, or even stop professing Jesus, but we live most of the week like God is irrelevant. Soon we live as if we don't need the redemption that Jesus provided on the cross. We sing "Amazing Grace" with gusto but don't recognize our own need for that same grace. Until we renounce our imagined control over what life sends our way and confess our own brokenness, we will never experience the abundant life Jesus provides—we will never inherit the revolutionary kingdom.

Jesus paints a vivid picture of what this self-renunciation looks like in the parable of the prodigal son in Luke 15. In the story, the younger son collected his inheritance early and headed off to the big city to make his own way—self-reliant and self-sufficient. Too many bad decisions later, the prodigal found himself slopping and eating with pigs. His illusion of control was stripped away as he awakened to his own powerlessness. He finally returned home, poor in spirit, planning to offer himself to his father as a hired servant. "While he was still a long way off, his father saw him and was moved with compassion. His father ran to his son, hugged him, and kissed him" (Luke 15:20). The son found no judgment, only love and acceptance. He discovered his legitimacy didn't come through what he had done; his legitimacy was based on who he was as a beloved son. Our efforts to create our own happiness, like the prodigal, may bring temporary comfort. But it's in the renunciation of self that our lives are transformed as we return to our Father's fold.

As a longtime pastor, I would like to think I have this self-renunciation piece down. But it's an ongoing struggle. I wince as I think back on those times when I have been all about self-determination even while proclaiming Jesus.

In 2003, for instance, I was asked by a national church leadership conference being hosted in Dallas to participate as a workshop presenter. As a workshop presenter, I could expect a smaller audience than as a speaker and no honorarium. I would also be responsible for covering my own travel. The only material benefit would be free admission to the rest of the conference. Now, there was a time when I would have been flattered to receive such an invite. However, a few short years before this invitation, I had been the "flavor of the month" church leadership speaker, headlining large conferences in major venues across the country.

Reminding myself "I am Christ's servant," I reluctantly agreed to lead the workshop. Then I found out that the conference host had also engaged our Ginghamsburg creative director Kim Miller, the

Ginghamsburg music team, and our video producer to help—but they were all getting paid! I remember blowing off steam about it in Kim's office before stalking away to call the conference host. Kim tried to stop me with, "Mike, don't do this; this is not who you are." But I persisted and made the call, using a choice profanity or two, and naming my demands for pay, travel reimbursement, and recognition. The host graciously agreed.

I would like to say I repented immediately, but I didn't. It was not until the next morning when I was meditating on God's Word that I admitted to myself, "You ass!" I called my contact back, offered my heartfelt apology, removed my demands from the previous day, and ultimately did the workshop for free. Literally, the only thing I received for my efforts was a T-shirt, while the rest of my staff team was well paid.

This self-renunciation stuff is not easy, but until we admit our own poverty and brokenness, we will never experience Kingdom wealth and whole life health.

BLESSED ARE THOSE WHO MOURN

> *"Blessed are those who mourn,*
> *for they will be comforted."*
>
> (Matthew 5:4 NIV)

The kingdom of heaven is an upside-down kingdom. The Beatitudes remind us that often, to go forward, we first have to go back. We must lose ourselves to find ourselves. In essence the second beatitude declares, "Blessed are those who face and embrace their pain."

And we don't have to exist in this world very long before pain starts to have an impact. We enter the world as children with open, soft hearts. We have the expectation that life is supposed to be fair, that good should always come our way. All too soon we are confronted with the reality of a broken world.

As I write this, I am preparing for my fifty-year high school reunion. How is that even possible? I am amazed how much high school reunions can affect your psyche, no matter how old you are or how much you have accomplished in life. At class reunions, you can start feeling like an awkward fifteen-year-old again. You are reunited with people who have no understanding of your life since high school commencement. But they remember all too well the failures of your youth.

At each reunion I've attended, one woman who was always part of my graduating class's "in" crowd has inevitably approached me to ask, "Do you remember the time in second grade when you wet your pants in the lunch room? The lunch room monitor Mrs. So-and-So made you stand in a green wastebasket in the middle of the lunchroom until you dried out." In an instant, I am returned to that moment of extreme humiliation from sixty years ago. In the expanse of my life, it was one tiny blip on the radar screen, yet the pain can be as instantly real to me today as it was in 1959.

I would wager each of us can remember similar painful moments from our childhood. Do you remember the first time that you were ever excluded from a group or made fun of as a kid? Do you remember overhearing your soon-to-be-divorced parents arguing in the next room? It doesn't take long for those open, tender hearts we were born with to harden. We develop a shell that's more difficult to fracture. We withdraw and seek isolation, unwilling to risk vulnerability. We begin to convince ourselves we can't be loved for who we really are. At the root of our isolation is pain, and the fruit it produces is shame. Often addictive behaviors are fueled by our failure to face and embrace the pain from our past. We start trying to be who we think others want us to be, instead of living into the fullness of the people God designed us to be. Worse yet, we can deflect our own pain and begin to shame others so we can temporarily feel better about ourselves.

Public shaming isn't new. In early America, Puritans used to throw people into the stocks in the town square for a day or two of public humiliation. We now post "shame" on social media where it lives forever—or at least until Jesus comes back. As parent advocate Sue Scheff notes, "Just a generation ago, an embarrassing gaffe might have been written up in the local paper or gossiped about over backyard fences until it was old news. But today is much different. The Internet has eternal life and boundless reach, and victims of a digital disaster must learn to live forever with the implications of that high-tech 'tattoo.'"[3] Politics has always been a brutal sport, but the sheer negative name-calling alone has reached new heights—more appropriately, "new depths"—since the start of the 2016 presidential election cycle. Is it any wonder that, in 2018, the CDC reported suicide rates were rising in nearly every state in the nation?[4]

How many times are we convinced Jesus couldn't possibly love us or others as we are? The world tells us we aren't beautiful, wealthy, or successful enough to matter. We will never appear on a *Forbes Magazine* list of the top ten anything. We will always be that little humiliated kid who stood in a trash can in the middle of a crowded elementary school lunch room. So we struggle to become something we are not—to reach a perfection we will never attain on our own, no matter how many "how to" articles we read, pithy tweets we make, or staged Instagram photos we post.

Jesus—not the world—offers the antidote. Christ alone extends amazing grace, inviting us to release our false beliefs and reimagine our lovability. When we turn to Christ, we trade our places of pain, shame, and brokenness for comfort and blessedness. When we embrace the love of Christ for ourselves, we are also far less likely to remain in the blame and shame game that wounds the spirits and lives of others.

BLESSED ARE THE MEEK

> "Blessed are the meek,
>   for they will inherit the earth."
>   (Matthew 5:5 NIV)

While those the culture calls "powerful" engage in saber-rattling, economic retaliation, and government shutdowns to bend others to their will, or tweet boastfully about who would win a fistfight with whom, Jesus stands on a hillside touting the virtue of being meek. What gives?

In my pre-Christian days, I perceived Christians as weak and boring. I thought all Christians were like vanilla ice cream. Now some people like vanilla ice cream, but I can't imagine walking into

Graeter's (my all-time favorite ice cream shop) and ordering vanilla. What I learned after my conversion is the meek are far from weak, and the meek will inherit the earth.

Jesus himself is the first and perfect example. In the final days of his human existence, Jesus stood before the Roman prefect Pontius Pilate, beaten and bloodied, to be judged. Jesus was perceived as a seditious revolutionary, a threat to both Jewish religious leaders and the Roman government. Despite his access to heaven's full power and resources, he stood quietly as he suffered injustice, meek but not weak, allowing himself to be convicted and executed for the Kingdom's sake.

Other historical figures would later model this same strong meekness to bring about world change, notably Mahatma Gandhi, Martin Luther King Jr., and Nelson Mandela. Gandhi stood against the entire British Empire, without weapons, to earn India's independence from Britain. Martin Luther King Jr. led a nonviolent resistance movement that would transform civil rights in the US, though it eventually cost him his life. Nelson Mandela, the South African anti-apartheid revolutionary, political leader, and philanthropist, endured twenty-seven unjust years in prison only to emerge as the key force for ending the racist system of apartheid. These three men faced insurmountable odds, yet all three won their revolutions. They mastered the weapons of the Spirit. Each of them showed love will always win against hate, vulnerability will always be victorious against control, and the Spirit will always win against the flesh.

Jesus said, "You have heard that it was said, *An eye for an eye and a tooth for a tooth.* But I say to you that you must not oppose those who want to hurt you. If people slap you on the right cheek, you must turn the left cheek to them as well" (Matthew 5:38-39). If you can act like that, you will inherit the earth. If you can choose to turn the other cheek when persecuted, you are ultimately more powerful than the Osama Bin Ladens of the world, for you cannot be broken and bullied. "When they wish to haul you to court and take your shirt, let them have your coat too. When they force you to go one mile, go with them two. Give to those who ask, and don't refuse those who wish to borrow from you" (Matthew 5:40-42). The meek are not the weak.

Kingdom power little resembles what we consider to be earthly power. In the revolutionary kingdom, it's not those who "lord it over others" who are great, but those who serve under the Lordship of Christ. Jesus said it best:

> *"You know that those who rule the Gentiles show off their authority over them and their high-ranking officials order them around. But that's not the way it will be with you. Whoever wants to be great among you will be your servant. Whoever wants to be first among you will be your slave— just as the Human One didn't come to be served but rather to serve and to give his life to liberate many people.*
> *(Matthew 20:25-28)*

How much more quickly would the kingdom of God come to Planet Earth if those who walked the "halls of power" in our country and beyond understood the true definition of what it means to be a "public servant!"

BLESSED ARE THOSE WHO HUNGER AND THIRST FOR RIGHTEOUSNESS

> *"Blessed are those who hunger and thirst for righteousness,*
> *for they will be filled."*
> *(Matthew 5:6 NIV)*

Right now we live in a world that is always hungry and thirsty. The problem is the world is trying to satisfy its hunger and thirst with the wrong things.

We were created to be in right relationship with God, but because of sin and brokenness, we try to fill the void with whatever comes to mind or is conveniently at hand at that moment—our favorite Netflix series, sex, junk food, shopping, power plays, money. But righteousness only comes from a life that is intentionally lived to please the Father—a life of right actions, attitudes, and accountability. Righteousness is not about being the best, but about giving God our best daily. It is not about being perfect, but about striving for perfection in the midst of our brokenness. We begin to be transformed when we can laugh at our past, grasp that God is healing us in the present, and believe God is setting us up for a promising future.

As I write these words, we've recently celebrated the start of a new year. Once again, it was easy for my news app and social media feeds to lead me in wrong directions for fulfilling my hunger and thirst. Headlines tempted me with suggestions like, "5 Great Car Accessories on Sale Right Now," "How to Lose Weight the Healthy Way in the New Year," and "19 Movies to Binge during Your New Year's Day Hangover." I love cars, and my Instagram feed somehow magically knows it. Ads for the BMW Z4 roadster and the Mercedes-Benz XL 500 are daily features. Any or all of these things might be worthwhile, but they will never assuage my deepest hunger and thirst.

How have you bought into fallible solutions instead of heeding Jesus' call: "desire first and foremost God's kingdom and God's righteousness, and all these things will be given to you as well" (Matthew 6:33)?

BLESSED ARE THE MERCIFUL

> "Blessed are the merciful,
> for they will be shown mercy."
> (Matthew 5:7 NIV)

I believe this beatitude and the one before it go together. Righteousness needs to be balanced by mercy, for righteousness without mercy becomes self-righteousness.

Sadly, self-righteous people are the ugliest people I know. Self-righteous people never unpack their suitcase and truly move into the revolutionary kingdom. Self-righteous folk do all the right things, but for all the wrong reasons. They read their Bible. They go to church. They mount that little fish symbol on the back of their car and post a daily Scripture with a pretty background on Facebook.

But all of their actions are about proving to God and proclaiming to others that they can be more righteous than other people. No. None of us is righteous. None of us can measure up to God. That's why we need the mercy God provides at Jesus' cross before we can take up residency in the revolutionary kingdom. Righteousness needs the balance of mercy, and mercy needs the boundaries of righteousness.

Mercy is not a sentimental emotion; it is the heart of God in action. In Luke 10, an expert in the law, who wanted to prove to Jesus he was loving his neighbor as himself, asked Jesus, "And who is my neighbor?" (verse 29). Jesus responded with one of the greatest illustrations of mercy in the Bible, the parable of the good Samaritan.

Jesus told the story of a man traveling from Jerusalem to Jericho who was beaten and stripped by robbers. A priest traveling the same road saw the injured man but passed by on the other side of the road, no doubt thinking about the next sermon he needed to deliver or the potluck church dinner in the church fellowship hall he planned to preside over for his flock. Soon another religious leader passed by, and he didn't stop to help, either. How easy it is to do all the right things for all the wrong reasons. Righteousness without mercy easily becomes a dead, self-righteous religion. Finally, a Samaritan, whose religious practices, if he had any, would have been considered seriously suspect by the two religious leaders, encountered the injured man and took pity on him. The Samaritan's emotion was accompanied by intentional action. He bandaged the victim, then transported him to an inn, set him up with ongoing care, and footed the entire bill.

After concluding the parable, Jesus asked his original questioner, "Which one of these three was a neighbor to the man who encountered thieves?" (verse 36). The expert in the law responded, "The one who demonstrated mercy toward him" (verse 37). As Jesus told the expert, we must "[g]o and do likewise" (verse 37).

In a world that defines political power as sorting people into winners' and losers' columns, we too often expect mercy for ourselves with little effort or desire to extend it to others.

Blessed Are the Pure in Heart

> *"Blessed are the pure in heart,*
> *for they will see God."*
> *(Matthew 5:8 NIV)*

Practicing religion can be a lot like decorating Christmas trees. Now, I love Christmas trees. Even now, in my seventh decade of life, a little bit of the kid in me comes out when we put up our tree after Thanksgiving. At night I like to turn off all other lights in the house and just soak in the lighted reflections of that festive tree. It's beautiful and vibrant—until you get up close. Then you start to see the truth. Whether it's a tree you cut down or an artificial one you bought at the big box store, it's dead. It's strictly ornamental. No matter how beautiful it is in this moment, it will never produce fruit. Any apples we find hanging from its branches are inevitably fake.

The Beatitudes remind us that, ultimately, faith is a matter of the heart, a matter of our inner being. We can think of them as "be-attitudes" instead of "do-attitudes." In the world, we place value on what we do and how we look on the outside, ignoring the fact that what is on the inside will eventually become visible as well. The first question we often ask when we meet a new person is, "So, what do you do?" We patiently snap twenty shots with our cell phone to find the perfect shot for our profile pic (and then try every filter our phone offers, determined to find the most flattering one). If only we put that much effort into the work of the heart!

God's Word reminds us, "Above all else, guard your heart, / for everything you do flows from it" (Proverbs 4:23 NIV). Jesus frequently called out the heart issues of some religious leaders in his day: "How terrible it will be for you legal experts and Pharisees. Hypocrites! You are like whitewashed tombs. They look beautiful on the outside. But inside they are full of dead bones and all kinds of filth" (Matthew 23:27).

Our heart passions, whether we admit to them or not, are far more powerful than our stated beliefs. I have never met a person who "believes in" adultery. I have never met a person who "believes in" addiction. Most of the things we do that we don't like about ourselves—and all of us could make a list of those things—are not a matter of having wrong beliefs. We overeat; we overspend; we lie; we cheat. Why? Whatever we allow to take hold and grow in our hearts soon controls us. We want to keep our private life and our "God life" separate and parallel. Would you or I be the first to volunteer if God offered to show our private life from the past week on a big screen in the church sanctuary during Sunday worship?

Jesus said, "No one can serve two masters" (Matthew 6:24). Whatever we allow to grow on the inside of us is going to become visible on the outside. As soon as I spot a questionable mole on my body, I'm calling the doctor. I don't tolerate cancer; I eradicate it. As a Jesus-follower, I need to be as vigilant about unresolved issues within the heart that could soon become a cancerous darkness.

Pride can be a troublesome area of darkness for many. Left unchecked, it leads me to believe in God without living as though I really need God. I can proclaim Christ on Sunday and then live like hell the rest of the week. James refers to this way of life as being double-minded, adding, "People like that should never imagine that they will receive anything from the Lord. They are double-minded, unstable in all their ways" (James 1:7-8). Our thoughts become actions; our actions become our life patterns; our life patterns become our destiny. Sow a thought and reap an eternity.

Cancer is a tough disease to beat on your own. Similarly, transformation of the heart requires a cross. It takes me less than twenty-four hours to lose the fear of God. Daily I need to work my program, acknowledging my sin before God, not allowing any area of my heart to go unexposed. I need to practice the five daily life disciplines, or D.R.I.V.E., I write about in the book *Momentum for Life*: daily devotion to God, readiness for lifelong learning, investing in key relationships, visioning for the future, and eating and exercising for health. I can't afford to take a day off. We also need other Jesus-followers with us on the journey for accountability and encouragement, people who proclaim and practice a revolutionary kingdom-of-God worldview.

BLESSED ARE THE PEACEMAKERS

"Blessed are the peacemakers,
for they will be called children of God."
(Matthew 5:9 NIV)

The Hebrew word for peace is *shalom*, which means "wholeness." Peace doesn't mean the absence of trouble. Peace means experiencing wholeness or well-being in spite of the circumstance you find yourself in. I can be in a financial storm, I can be in a relational storm, I can be in a personal storm, but I still can experience the welfare, the wholeness, the well-being of God, even in the midst of those storms. Our peace, our wholeness, does not depend on the circumstances of life.

Note that the word Jesus uses in Matthew 5:9 is *peacemaker*, not *peacekeeper*. It's easy to do the latter, but it requires risk to do the former. Peacekeepers are consumed with avoiding conflict, which can lead to codependent behavior. Peacemakers actively persist in bringing about God's desired outcomes. Jesus identified his role as peacemaker when he proclaimed his mission statement:

"'The Spirit of the Lord is upon me,
  because the Lord has anointed me.
He has sent me to preach good news to the poor,
  to proclaim release to the prisoners
  and recovery of sight to the blind,
  to liberate the oppressed."
(Luke 4:18)

Peacemakers are barrier breakers who tear down the walls that divide. They are disciples walking in the dust of their rabbi who actively intervene on behalf of those who are poor, misused, or powerless.

Peacemakers confront the powerful when the powerful use their position to abuse or oppress. Peacemakers speak truth in love to those who are destroying their lives with destructive and addictive behaviors. Peacemakers stand in the gap for families at the US and Mexican border when children are snatched from parents' arms.

Peacemakers refuse to remain silent in the presence of ageism, sexism, racism, classism, or any other "-ism" that denigrates and divides God's people. Peacemakers build bridges, not barriers. In the next two chapters we will explore further our opportunities for being God's force for Shalom in a deeply troubled world.

BLESSED ARE THE PERSECUTED

> *"Blessed are those who are persecuted because of*
> *righteousness,*
>   *for theirs is the kingdom of heaven.*
>
> *"Blessed are you when people insult you, persecute you*
> *and falsely say all kinds of evil against you because of me.*
> *Rejoice and be glad, because great is your reward in heaven,*
> *for in the same way they persecuted the prophets who were*
> *before you."*
>
>   *(Matthew 5:10-12 NIV)*

When we step into God's mission, when we make a commitment to put our behinds on the line and become part of God's peace-making force in the world, we need to expect persecution. Scripture assures us everyone who wants to live a godly life in Christ Jesus will be persecuted. Everyone. No exceptions. Everyone who commits himself or herself to the mission of Jesus goes into the world with a target on his or her back—and the attack can often come from unexpected sources.

Karl Barth was a Swiss theologian, whose work in its entirety is said to be comparable to that of Augustine and Aquinas. He was shocked and dismayed when he saw theology professors he had studied under and admired openly supporting the German Kaiser's war efforts in the lead-up to World War I. This development spurred him to a deeper study of the Bible and some of his greatest theological works. He also refused to be co-opted by the Nazis during the rise of Adolf Hitler. Despite the risk, he served as the primary author of the Barmen Declaration, a 1934 call for Christian resistance against the theological claims of Nazism. It cost him his teaching chair at Bonn University.[5] Barth's fellow pastor and theologian Dietrich

Bonhoeffer, who also resisted the Nazis' false theology and who took the risk of participating in a plot to assassinate Hitler, was executed by the German state in the Flossenburg concentration camp in 1945.

Ephesians 6:12 says, "We aren't fighting against human enemies but against rulers, authorities, forces of cosmic darkness, and spiritual powers of evil in the heavens." As soon as you make a commitment to live a godly life in Christ Jesus, evil will have the intent to disrupt the purposes of God in your life.

It may sound crazy, but persecution is a privilege to be not only expected but embraced: "Rejoice and be glad, because great is your reward in heaven, for in the same way they persecuted the prophets who were before you" (Matthew 5:12 NIV).

The cost of persecution can be great. Gandhi and Mandela were jailed. Martin Luther King Jr. was shot. Jesus went to the cross. So why again is persecution a privilege?

First, persecution serves to open the eyes of others. As a young child, I watched the evening news with my parents on our family's black-and-white television set. Coverage many nights featured stories about the Civil Rights Movement. Seeing law enforcement turn German shepherd dogs loose on elderly men and women who were peacefully protesting left an indelible impression. I would not be who I am today if I had not witnessed these and other injustices.

Persecution also drives us to pray. Jesus prayed so fervently on the night of his arrest, his sweat was like drops of blood (Luke 22:44). When I experience pain in my life, I realize I'm powerless when I attempt to operate solely out of my own strength. I am reminded I must surrender to God what I am unable to do on my own.

Persecution also provides a powerful opportunity for praise. It teaches me to speak God's possibilities in all circumstances, not despair. As E. Stanley Jones wrote, Christ "transforms hate into hallelujahs and misery into melody."[6]

Finally, persecution teaches us the Kingdom value of perseverance. Jesus declared, "The one who endures to the end will be delivered" (Matthew 24:13). Nelson Mandela endured twenty-seven years of imprisonment in South Africa because of his resistance to the apartheid system. He walked out of prison undefeated to resume the cause and was subsequently elected the first black president of South Africa. Under his leadership, the nation started the healing process of reconciliation. Mandela persevered; he endured.

As we will examine in the chapters ahead, never surrendering, always persevering, must become the hallmark of all who are firmly committed to the Lordship of Jesus Christ and to the efficacy of his revolutionary kingdom. There is too much at stake for any lesser commitment.

Chapter 5
Kingdom Economy

The Beatitudes starkly illustrate the contrast between the revolutionary kingdom of the Rebel Jesus and the politics of power on display daily in the broken world around us. The upside-down nature of the Kingdom also reveals itself in its economics.

The financial website Investopedia defines an economy as "the large set of inter-related production and consumption activities that aid in determining how scarce resources are allocated."[1] Although that's a helpful day-to-day definition, it also almost immediately reveals a conflict with God's economy. The earthly economy is built around the scarcity mentality; God's kingdom is built on abundance.

In our nation's capital right now, it seems almost all interactions are based on a win-lose strategy. As one website reminds us, "When choosing this strategy, one takes on an adversarial or competitive view. The focus is on achieving immediate goals, with little or no regard for building future relationships."[2]

This focus certainly explains why the federal government seems so broken to everyday folk. When the Democratic Party regained the House of Representatives in the 2018 midterm election, they not only won congressional seats but also won back the biggest offices, best committee appointments, and the speakership. Of course, the opposite happened each time Republicans wrested control of Congress. I am not naïve; this is how our political system works. But this win-lose strategy has become so dominant, almost nothing helpful or healthy can be accomplished. There seems to be no reward for cooperation across the aisle.

When a scarcity mentality serves as the basis for our interactions, my having something means you having less. My winning means you losing. There is never enough to go around, so we had better constantly scheme and strive to ensure we not only receive our fair share but also protect it from others. We put up fences to protect our property and walls to protect our borders—lines that in truth most likely remain invisible, or at least artificial, from God's vantage point.

Contrast the world's scarcity mentality with Kingdom abundance. Our sovereign God is a God of abundance, with "cattle upon a thousand hills" (Psalm 50:10), both literally and metaphorically. In God's revolutionary kingdom we experience abundance when we give our resources away, not when we hoard them.

Through the prophet Malachi, God promised to bless God's people when they made offerings in the rebuilt temple in Jerusalem:

> *Bring the whole tenth-part to the storage house so there*
> *might be food in my house.*
> * Please test me in this,*
> * says the LORD of heavenly forces.*
> *See whether I do not open all the windows of the heavens*
> *for you*
> * and empty out a blessing until there is enough.*
> *(Malachi 3:10)*

And Jesus said "Give, and it will be given to you. A good portion—packed down, firmly shaken, and overflowing—will fall into your lap. The portion you give will determine the portion you receive" (Luke 6:38). In God's economy, there is plenty for all when we live generously, with our hands open to others.

By no means is the Bible a treatise on economic systems, but we can find in it the genesis of much of what we see in economic systems today. Perhaps the most prevalent economic principle God's Word promotes, applicable to all of life, is the principle of sowing and reaping.

The apostle Paul declares, "Make no mistake, God is not mocked. A person will harvest what they plant" (Galatians 6:7). Both Old and New Testaments repeatedly teach this principle. When I am my best self for the Kingdom, I find it incredibly reassuring. Likewise, it fills me with a little trepidation when my selfish instincts squelch my generosity.

Some of us try to use Scripture to validate what we believe to be the best economic model in the world today. Capitalism, of course, is very near and dear to our American hearts. At the same time, some forms of socialism seem to be attracting attention from our younger generations.[3] A quick Google search will reveal research, blogs, and articles using Scripture to prove that God supports free market capitalism. Christian socialism, on the other hand, has its own Wikipedia entry, as does Christian communism.

Who to believe? It is above my pay grade to support or refute such arguments. I don't know enough, and also suspect I could find points I agree and disagree with in many of the conflicting arguments. But I do believe there are two Kingdom economic principles worth exploring that stand all too often in sharp contrast with our current cultural practices.

First, everything—and I do mean everything—belongs to God. We ultimately own nothing, while God gives us access to all we need through our willingness to be a resource to other people. Second, God's Kingdom design calls for economic justice—something else we are hard-pressed to find in the win-lose game we are currently playing. Let's examine each of these principles, first in the context of what God's Word says about them, then from the context of what the world practices.

It All Belongs to God

As we buy storage units to contain the overflow from our basements and garages, base part of our status on the car we drive or phone we carry, and keep others' hands away from what we perceive as our stuff, God declares, "It is all mine and to be used for my purposes." Psalm 24:1 reminds us, "The earth is the LORD's, and everything in it, / the world, and its inhabitants too." We aren't the owners of our money, time, or talents; we are the stewards of what God has generously provided. We are to use what the King has given us for Kingdom purposes for an ordained period of time, before the King asks for it back.

The perfect biblical illustration of this principle is Jesus' parable of the talents in Matthew 25:14-30. The man who was "leaving on a trip" represents God, who "called his servants and handed HIS possessions over to them" (verse 14, emphasis added). One servant received five valuable coins; another, two; and the final servant, one. Regardless of the number of coins received, the master expected his wealth would be invested (stewarded) wisely during his absence. Of course, when the master returned to collect his property, he praised two servants for doing just that. Both had doubled the initial amount they had received. But during the master's travels, the final servant had carefully tucked his coin away in the back of his climate-controlled, 24/7 security-monitored storage unit, under the mounds of the rest of his excess stuff. To say the returning master was displeased would be an understatement.

We are to invest and deploy what we have been given on behalf of others. We have to release it in order to increase it for the greater good. Joseph's story makes a great case study of this principle. Sold into slavery by his envious brothers, Joseph soon becomes a trusted servant to Potiphar, captain of Pharaoh's army in Egypt. He rises to the position of superintendent, or steward, over all Potiphar's household because of the faithful way he manages his master's resources for the greater good. When Joseph is falsely accused of sexually assaulting Potiphar's wife, he is placed in prison. So far, the law of sowing and reaping doesn't seem to be working in Joseph's favor! However, when prisoner Joseph is offered the opportunity to interpret Pharaoh's dreams and is able to do so under God's guidance, he is freed.

The dreams had revealed Egypt would experience seven years of plenty followed by seven years of famine. Although Joseph could have used that "insider trading" info from God to pursue some savvy market investments of his own so he could take future advantage of the Egyptians' looming misery, he instead invests his talents in devising and leading a plan to ensure Pharaoh and the people he rules will not go hungry. For the second time, Joseph grows trust with his previous captors by releasing the blessings of God to benefit the greater community. His efforts also position him to feed his own family, both the immediate one he had acquired in Egypt and his birth family, with whom the famine makes possible a reconciliation.

Our lives are not our own; our resources are not our own. Like Joseph, we are to invest the treasures that have been entrusted to us for God's purposes, not sit idly by as food deserts, lack of access to healthcare, and limited educational opportunities plague our less economically fortunate neighbors. We have a responsibility as kingdom-of-God people to act and invest on behalf of that Kingdom.

The Earth Matters

Being a faithful steward of the Master's property also means faithfully stewarding our most important resource of all—this planet we call home.

I confess I simply don't understand the propensity of some Christians to ignore environmental issues like climate change because they don't see those issues as faith-related concerns. Why don't they? As we've noted already, God owns the planet and all that exists on it. Scripture reveals God created it, loves and values it, sustains it, and redeems it. In return, creation testifies to the Creator and praises God.

Scripture leaves no doubt God created Earth and its life forms. Whether in seven 24-hour days, over seven God-sized days, or through some form of a "big bang," God created the world and is the Alpha and Omega of all. The very first verse of my Bible declares it: "In the beginning God created the heavens and the earth" (Genesis 1:1 NIV). And this isn't simply an Old Testament declaration. Paul writes to the Colossians,

> *The Son is the image of the invisible God,*
> *the one who is first over all creation,*

> *Because all things were created by him:*
> *both in the heavens and on the earth,*
> *the things that are visible and the things that are*
> *invisible.*
> *Whether they are thrones or powers*
> *or rulers or authorities,*
> *all things were created through him and for him.*
> *(Colossians 1:15-16)*

As I noted earlier, we begin to sense God's love for and value of creation in Genesis 1:31, when God observes all the new creation and declares it is "supremely good." Psalm 145:9 assures us, "The LORD is good to everyone and everything; / God's compassion extends to all his handiwork!" "In whose grasp is the life of every thing, / the breath of every person?" (Job 12:10). Paul confirms God's intention to redeem a fallen world extends to all of God's creation: "The whole creation waits breathless with anticipation for the revelation of God's sons and daughters. Creation was subjected to frustration, not by its own choice—it was the choice of the one who subjected it—but in the hope that the creation itself will be set free from slavery to decay and brought into the glorious freedom of God's children" (Romans 8:19-21).

In a sense, we see creation reciprocating God's love. Look at Psalm 19:1-2:

> *Heaven is declaring God's glory;*
> *the sky is proclaiming his handiwork.*
> *One day gushes the news to the next,*
> *and one night informs another what needs to be known.*

Creation testifies to God's glory and responds in joy to what God has done:

> *You will go out with celebration,*
> *and you will be brought back in peace.*
> *Even the mountains and the hills will burst into song*
> *before you;*
> *and all the trees of the field will clap their hands.*
> *(Isaiah 55:12)*

Some Christians discount the importance of the physical world through the "easy believe-ism" form of Christianity that has gripped so many of us: "If I say *this* prayer using *these* words, I can sit around waiting to go to heaven." No! As I have urged vehemently over the forty-plus years of my ministry, we *aren't* to sit around waiting to go to heaven. We are to actively serve as the conduits for bringing heaven's resources to Planet Earth. As I noted in my book *The Christian Wallet*, the earth *does* matter:

> That God is simply going to destroy the world anyway is also not what I read in my Bible. Isaiah 61:2-4, the passage I always note as being Jesus' mission statement (see Luke 4:17-19), indicates that in the "year of the LORD's favor," the redeemed poor, brokenhearted, captives, and prisoners will "rebuild the ancient ruins and restore the places long devastated; they will renew the ruined cities that have been devastated for generations" [Isaiah 61:4]. Note all the "re:" words—God is not starting over from scratch![4]

We must do more than avoid contributing to creation's destruction. God also, at the beginning of our existence, assigned us the task of actively stewarding creation. It was our first direct commandment from the Creator. Revisit Genesis 1:24-30 for a refresher. Proverbs reminds us, "Good people leave their grandchildren an inheritance" (Proverbs 13:22). I know of no more critical inheritance than a livable planet. As the grandfather of seven, I feel increasing urgency around this and, if I'm truthful, some increasing despair.

Many destructive disasters attributed in part to climate change marked the year 2018. A report by Christian Aid about the year's top ten most damaging disasters indicated each event alone causing over $1 billion of damage, with four events racking up more than $7 billion of damage each. Hurricane Florence incurred a price tag of $17 billion, with Hurricane Michael close behind at $15 billion. Those dollars reflect only insured losses. The totals would have been much higher if uninsured losses and lost productivity were factored in as well.

The top ten events ranged from devastating fires in California and floods in Japan and China to drought in Europe, Argentina, Australia, and South Africa. At the time I am writing this, 2019 is expected to be even hotter than 2018, which was the fourth hottest year on record.[5] I can only say I am grateful my grandkids all live in Ohio. This part of the Midwest has its own climate change consequences pending, but, for the short term, is less likely to experience the recurring devastation plaguing both coastlines, with regions of too much water on the East Coast, and low rainfall regions with not enough water on the West.

Clearly, climate change is a global problem. The United Nations issued a grim report in October 2018 with some important warnings. The U.N.'s Intergovernmental Panel on Climate Change described worsening food shortages, wildfires, and the mass die-off of coral reefs as soon as 2040. My oldest grandchild will be in her thirties in 2040 and may be mom by then to some of my great-grandkids. And who knows? I could even still be around. The scientists on the panel warned if the current rate of greenhouse gas emissions continues, the earth's atmosphere will warm by as much as 2.7 degrees Fahrenheit, putting coastlines at risk, pushing other regions into drought, reducing crop production, and ultimately increasing poverty. Animal life, plant life, biomes—all are at risk.[6]

How can Christians be so shortsighted as to not care about this issue? I find it ironic that some of us who define ourselves as political conservatives are often the first to deride the notion of climate change. How exactly did a concern for "conservation" get completely left out of our "conservative" political framework?

Often our ethnocentric, isolationist tendencies in the US lead us to view reports like this one as something that happens to somebody else, somewhere else. We can't hide behind that excuse this time. Shortly after the U.N. report was released, the Trump administration—not an administration known for being particularly friendly toward environmental causes—released its own dire report. It describes climate change's impacts on communities and the economy as well as on interconnected systems like water resources, food production, public health, and national security. The Summary Findings section alone was enough to make the hair on the back of my neck stand up. It stated conclusions like these:

- The impacts of climate change are already being felt in communities across the country.
- Future climate change is expected to further disrupt many areas of life, exacerbating existing challenges to prosperity posed by aging and deteriorating infrastructure, stressed ecosystems, and economic inequality.
- With continued growth in emissions at historic rates, annual losses in some economic sectors are projected to reach hundreds of billions of dollars by the end of the century— more than the current gross domestic product (GDP) of many US states.

And the report indicates that, as so often seems to be the case, "People who are already vulnerable, including lower-income and other marginalized communities, have lower capacity to prepare for and cope with extreme weather and climate-related events and are expected to experience greater impacts."[7]

Some of us attempt to cling to another fallacy: that we may have the economic means to ride out climate-change disasters or avoid its costs that plague other people. When I have been in places like Darfur, Sudan, I have shaken my head at the acres upon acres of land near the internally displaced persons' camps that seemed completely coated with discarded plastic bags. But I didn't have to remain overly troubled by it, since I was returning home and all the yards in my neighborhood are practically pristine.

My reaction raises two issues. First, Jesus calls me to make his mission statement my life's work:

The Spirit of the Lord is upon me,
    because the Lord has anointed me.
He has sent me to preach good news to the poor,
    to proclaim release to the prisoners

and recovery of sight to the blind,
to liberate the oppressed.

(Luke 4:18)

If it impacts the poor, it impacts me.

Second, climate change is coming after all of us, so to speak. It's easy for us to feel removed geographically and socioeconomically from the toll it takes on our remote sisters and brothers. For instance, we often think of drought as having the biggest impact on poor, rural areas located in arid parts of other continents. Yet, one of the worst droughts, continuing into 2019, has been in Cape Town, South Africa. Cape Town is South Africa's oldest city, with a population of over 4 million people. Other large cities with relatively high water risks include New Delhi, Beijing, Jakarta, Rome, San Francisco, the Manhattan area, and others.[8] Potentially, none of us are immune.

Doing Our Part

Proclaiming a problem without offering a solution is unhelpful. The overall challenge of climate change must be addressed by whole nations and whole peoples. But that doesn't let individuals completely off the hook by any means.

First, we Christians must stop sticking our heads in the sand. Climate change truly is a matter of life and death. Ignoring it or minimizing its existence is not going to make it go away. As unpleasant as you may find them, read the U.N. and US reports. You owe it to yourself and to future generations.

Second, be part of the solution instead of an additional contributor to the problem. Here are some things you and I can do, inspired by journalist Jeff McMahon's suggestions:

- Eat less meat. I love a good steak, but greenhouse gas emissions from animal agriculture contribute anywhere from 14.5 to 51 percent of total emissions, depending on which source you consult.
- Shop organic, if you have that option. Nonorganic food is grown in fertilizer that began as a byproduct of oil refining. Besides, when you eat organic, you consume fewer pesticides.

- Buy locally sourced products and foods when you can. The more we minimize transportation for goods we consume, the more we reduce emissions.
- Turn your thermostat down or up. No, we shouldn't have to freeze to death in cold winters, but keeping climate-controlled conditions at the perfect 70 degrees all year long is ultimately more costly than it is worth.
- Reduce, reuse, recycle.
- Walk when you can or use public transportation. Vehicles are not required for every journey.
- Do things the old-fashioned way. Clotheslines are nice.
- Did you know the U.N. has a tool for helping you offset your carbon emissions? Go to climateneutralnow.org. You can calculate your emissions and then contribute offsetting dollars toward projects you select that are reducing emissions and contributing to communities.[9]

We should also vote with not only our feet but also our vote! I am not asking anyone to be pro-Democratic, pro-Republican, or pro-Libertarian. Let's just be pro-God's economy and advocates for God's creation. Let's live as subjects of the revolutionary kingdom, not as win-lose partisans of rigid political platforms.

Kingdom Justice

As Jesus-followers, our ultimate aim should always be to proclaim God's glory. Injustice never glorifies God. God's economy as described in Scripture would not be considered socialism in its purest form. We do see private ownership throughout Scripture, with the important caveat that God ultimately owns everything. While taking care of ourselves and our families is certainly important, our resources are never intended to be used solely for our own support and enjoyment. Kingdom resources entrusted to our stewardship are to be multiplied and invested to serve the greater good.

The description of the early Christian church in Acts 2 is always my favorite example of such stewardship. There was private ownership, as implied in verse 46, which states believers broke bread together "in their homes." But they also sold and sacrificed what they needed to for the good of the whole community.

In Luke 12:16-21, Jesus tells the parable of a wealthy man whose grounds produced an amazing harvest. He decided to build bigger barns to hold his wealth so he could retire early, kick back, and enjoy life. Let's just say God was disgusted by the wealthy man's intentions. When I read this parable, I receive no sense God was unhappy about the man's property or wealth itself; instead, his selfishness was his downfall. The man uses the word "I" six times in three sentences before he threw in a "you"—but even that is a reference to himself, in the second person.

God's economy calls us to self-sacrifice and generosity. Remember: We are God's conduit for bringing heaven's resources to Planet Earth. We are to be producers of blessings in others' lives, not consumers of stuff. Hoarding our abundant wealth in God's economy is a recipe for disaster. Take a look at Ecclesiastes 5:12-14:

> *Sweet is the worker's sleep, whether there's a lot or little to*
> *eat; but the excess of the wealthy won't let them sleep.*
>
> *I have seen a sickening tragedy under the sun: people hoard*
> *their wealth to their own detriment. Then that wealth is lost*
> *in a bad business venture so that when they have children,*
> *they are left with nothing.*

God's economy requires economic justice, as these verses from Isaiah demonstrate:

> *Isn't this the fast I choose:*
> *   releasing wicked restraints, untying the ropes of a yoke,*
> *   setting free the mistreated,*
> *   and breaking every yoke?*
> *Isn't it sharing your bread with the hungry*
> *   and bringing the homeless poor into your house,*
> *   covering the naked when you see them . . .*
> *Then . . . your own righteousness will walk before you.*
>
> *   (Isaiah 58:6-8)*

We are our brothers' and our sisters' keepers. We are expected to defend and deliver the defenseless, to provide a handout in emergencies and a hand up for future economic wholeness:

> *Give justice to the lowly and the orphan;*
> *maintain the right of the poor and the destitute!*
> *Rescue the lowly and the needy.*
> *Deliver them from the power of the wicked!*
>
> *(Psalm 82:3-4)*

The Problem of Wealth Inequality

Our worldly economies are really broken because they work for a few, not for all. Worse yet, we tend to blame those who struggle and fail to keep up rather than the systems that created their hardships. As Maia Szalavitz, a journalist who covers neuroscience stories for major publications, notes, we tend to practice something called "fundamental attribution error," which is the human tendency to see others' behavior "as being determined by their character—while excusing our own behavior based on circumstances." She uses an example of becoming unemployed and struggling to find work. If it happens to us, we see ourselves as innocent victims of bad luck who are working hard to find a new job. But we tend to view others who aren't employed as slackers. Their stories remain hidden to us, and we don't bother to find out the truth. The struggle is real; we too often just choose to ignore it.[10]

Shannon Davidson is a member of the Ginghamsburg Church family. She is a single mom with two sons who works full-time at a preschool/childcare center and attends school at night to pursue a medical coding certification. She also has to rely on rent subsidies, state-provided food assistance (formerly known as food stamps), Medicaid, tuition grants, and the kindness of others within the church to keep her family under a roof and fed, while at night she strives for future economic independence. Other people who see Shannon paying with an Ohio Direction Card/EBT in the grocery checkout line can find it very easy to view her as simply another welfare mom lazily relying on the government dole (otherwise known as our hard-earned tax dollars) because she lacks ambition. Nothing could be further from the truth.

We will return to Shannon's story later, because it also reflects what the people of the revolutionary kingdom can and should be doing on a personal level to help bring economic justice to the Shannons of the world. But first, let's rip the bandage off and take a closer look at current inequalities.

Time Magazine recently reported the US may be the world's richest country, but nearly one in five American children live in households considered to be food insecure.[11] Wow! Shame on us that in a land of wealth, 20 percent of our kids go to bed hungry at night and wake up just as hungry the next morning.

You may have heard it said the rich get richer and the poor get poorer. That's not just a familiar saying—it happens to be true. Around the world, the richest 1 percent of the world's people own half the world's wealth. To be more precise, the wealthiest people own 50.1 percent of the wealth, a figure that's up from 45.5 percent in 2001. This is a staggering inequity. The US has the most millionaires, with 15.3 million people worth at least one million or more.[12] I suppose, in a sense, 15.3 million sounds reassuringly large. But contrast that number with the total U.S. population of 325.7 million people. You'll realize most Americans aren't doing nearly so well.

Clearly, if 20 percent of our kids are food insecure, growing economic inequality is an American concern as well as a global one. The Economic Policy Institute has reported the wealthiest families in the US, the so-called "one percenters," took home twenty-five times more income than the rest of the population in 2015. And it seems like the gap just continues to grow, impacting all parts of the country, not just urban areas.[13]

As we look at these statistics, perhaps many of us are thinking, "Heck, I'm no millionaire. I'm one of those poor Joes or Janes being victimized by these economic inequalities myself." For some of us, that may certainly be true. However, many of us are actually wealthier than we think. In the fall of 2018, each person who made $32,400 a year belonged to the top 1 percent of the world's wealthiest people, based strictly on income. Now, it's a little tougher to crack the top 1 percent globally if you consider total wealth and not just income. In 2018, you would still qualify for the global 1 percent if everything you owned, including the equity in your home, had a net worth of $770,000. That threshold probably eliminates most of us. At the same time, by the world's standards, many of us in the US are amazingly comfortable, if not always appreciative of our privileged status.[14]

Rising wealth inequality in the US knocked approximately five percentage points off of the GDP per capita from 1990 to 2010. Not surprisingly, inequality also made it more difficult for children from the bottom 40 percent of US households to have access to educational opportunities, which in turn limited their access to future employment offering a livable wage. Eventually, billionaire owners of companies could find it difficult to find enough prospective customers who can afford to purchase their products.[15] Increases in US property crime, violent crime rates globally, and even drug-related deaths have also been linked to increasing economic disparities between the haves and have-nots.

Of course setting all this aside, just the sheer number of hungry kids alone in the US should grab Christians' attention.

As I write these words, the US is experiencing the longest government shutdown in its history. Yet many of our elected officials claim they can completely identify with unpaid federal employees who are struggling to keep their families housed, fed, and healthy. These "public servants" in many cases are millionaires, along with at least one self-proclaimed billionaire or two. We must pull off our blinders to the economic injustices sending our kids to bed hungry at night in one of the world's wealthiest nations.

How do we start to live and act out of the abundance of the revolutionary kingdom versus the fearful or selfish scarcity mentality of the unjust economics surrounding us?

ONE LIFE AT A TIME

Like climate change, broken economic systems and wealth inequality are global and national issues that must be addressed at a systemic level in order to fix them. Yet there are things we can do as Jesus-followers to become part of a solution.

Once again, let's open our eyes to the economic injustices around us and politically engage. I will not tell you how to vote in terms of any policy or specific politician. But I will encourage you to actively research and engage on a political level. Minimum wage arguments, tax code changes, segregation by neighborhoods, educational opportunities, healthcare access, and more are important arenas where we need to study, discern, pray, and vote as to how the Spirit of God's revolutionary kingdom leads us.

As individuals, we must also be intercessors on a very personal level. Let's return to Shannon Davidson's story, the single mom who, since her divorce in 2015, is like so many other parents in this country who work and receive government program assistance but still struggle to have enough money for the month. Yet in Shannon's case, God's intervention through the Ginghamsburg Church family has made all the difference.

At the time of her divorce, Shannon, who had previously provided in-home childcare to supplement her household income, was working two part-time jobs and earning an income completely inadequate for supporting herself and two sons. She started attending Ginghamsburg Church through her connections with a vibrant Mom2Mom ministry that supported her and helped her see new possibilities for her life. While attending Ginghamsburg, she committed her life to Christ.

An acquaintance at the church referred her to the open full-time preschool/childcare position Shannon currently holds, which provides more income and a stable schedule.

A car dealership owner who attends Ginghamsburg helped her replace the 1997 fuel-consuming fifteen-passenger van she had used for home day care with a newer, reliable, more efficient car for a fourth of what it would have normally cost.

A US Air Force veteran, another single mother who is professionally employed, asked Shannon what her dream was for leaving poverty behind. She suggested and cheerleads the medical coding opportunity Shannon is now pursuing.

One December, a complete Christmas dinner and gifts for Shannon and her sons showed up at the door.

Perhaps most importantly, an anonymous donor or family at Ginghamsburg gives her $400 each month like clockwork, an amount almost enough to meet her $519 monthly rent.

Without all of this, life for the Davidson family would be significantly different. When I spoke with Shannon about her story, she volunteered that the word she had selected to be her word for 2019 was "inspire." Shannon says her greatest future dream at this point is to reach the place, one day, where she is able to extend grace and opportunity to others in the same way it has been extended to her.

Who are the Shannons around you or your church who could experience some sense of Kingdom justice through your handouts, when needed, and your hand up for future prosperity and health?

Following the Rebel Jesus means being God's hands, feet, voice, and bank account for the oppressed and underserved. If each of us will begin to actively live out the renegade gospel in all its implications, we will be the bringers of God's revolutionary kingdom on Planet Earth, even if it happens one life—one Shannon—at a time.

Chapter 6
The "All In"

Have you ever read an exciting thriller or horror novel and skipped to the end of the book to see if your favorite character survived? Peeking at the last few pages removes the surprise factor of reaching the end one page at a time, but knowing the outcome can relieve a little stress along the way on the reading journey.

When I jump ahead to the end of the Bible and read Revelation, I am always relieved to see God's church ends up the same way it started out—with all people represented. When the apostle John describes his vision of God's throne in Revelation 7, he notes, "I looked, and there was a great crowd that no one could number. They were from every nation, tribe, people, and language. They were standing before the throne" (verse 9). I'm going to take John at his word and assume *every* actually means "every."

Now turn back with me to the birth of the church on the Day of Pentecost in Acts 2, when "there were pious Jews from every nation under heaven" present (verse 5). Can we once again assume *every* means "every"? Christ came to tear down the barriers dividing us from one another. So why do we keep rebuilding them? The church should be safe space from the "-isms" of racism, sexism, ageism, and classism that foster everything from fear to hate crimes. But too often we faithful church attenders can be as divisive in our actions and attitudes as an unchurched neighbor with a Confederate flag decal on his car window. We allow fear to trump faith. We fear those who don't look, speak, act, vote, love, or believe the same way we do.

I believe our ingrained cultural scarcity mentality also fuels some of our fear. If the Pakistani immigrant who lives down the street from us has had the temerity to open her own successful small business, we sometimes respond as if her success has robbed us, or another "fellow American" (who in our mind's eye looks and speaks a lot like we do), of work and income. Somehow, we conflate the immigrant's success with someone else's lost opportunity, possibly our own. If the Pakistani woman "has," then someone else has not. How quickly we forget God's economy is built on abundance.

I also believe our penchant for clinging to the "letter of the law" helps drive divisiveness. For as much as we like to sing and think about the words of "Amazing Grace," you'd think we would be better at claiming their meaning for our own lives and extending that same grace to others. We say we follow the Living Word, but we live by the law, focusing on publicly proving our worth. We go to church, read our Bible (or at least leave it out in plain sight on the coffee table), throw a twenty-dollar bill in the offering plate, vote for the preferred party platform at every election, and speak English as our primary language. In other words, we practice the "I don't drink, and I don't chew, and I don't go with folks who do" mantra in an effort to prove we are better than our neighbors who are different than we are.

As the miracle that occurred on the first Christian Pentecost demonstrates, the Kingdom is to be inclusive, not exclusive. We forget the decision about who's in and who's out is not ours to make. As Jesus reminds us in one of his parables, when the servants asked if they should pull up the weeds growing in the midst of the master's wheat crop, the master replied, "No, because if you gather the weeds, you'll pull up the wheat along with them. Let both grow side by side until the harvest" (Matthew 13:29-30).

Culture focuses on walls that divide. The revolutionary kingdom focuses on destroying walls. Being a citizen of the Kingdom means rejecting the ugly "-isms" cluttering our cultural landscape. If that's the case, why do younger generations perceive the church as fostering judgment and division?

I was recently talking with a friend's twenty-eight-year-old millennial son. He had attended Ginghamsburg Church with his family in his tween and teen years. He has a deep appreciation for what he has witnessed, since he was nine years old, as Ginghamsburg's continuing commitment to serve with people who are poor and oppressed. However, when he talks about American Christianity at large, his distaste quickly becomes apparent. "It's too political and too wrapped up in an unhealthy conservativism, promoting policies that are anything but Christlike." In other words, to my young friend the church little resembles the Savior it professes to worship.

Evangelical Relativism?

When I was a young pastor, I used to bemoan how evangelical Christians, and I considered myself one, were portrayed in the press and popular culture. Evangelicals were described as morally rigid, stiff and unyielding, firmly placing people, events, and cultural phenomena into right or wrong, black or white columns in our Christian ledgers. Dana Carvey's hilarious portrayal of The Church Lady on NBC's *Saturday Night Live* in the late 1980s provides the perfect visual.

Now, however, evangelicals are increasingly likely to be accused of moral relativism. We appear to be warming ourselves at the enemy's fire, just as Peter did after Jesus' arrest (Luke 22:55), setting the stage for Christ's crucifixion all over again. We are considered only too happy to become political bedmates with any politician or cause for the sake of expediency, as long as it promotes a narrow spectrum of core issues near and dear to the evangelical heart.

As reporter Eugene Scott noted in an analysis piece in *The Washington Post*, Jerry Falwell Jr. has called President Trump, who would have been an unlikely choice for evangelical support by evangelicals' past standards, "a dream president." Scott also observed, "For many evangelical voters, moving America forward means continuing to support the most antiabortion candidate regardless of his track record on any other moral issue." Scott went on to cite white evangelical support for Senate candidate Roy Moore in a 2017 special election in Alabama as a case in point, despite the allegations of Moore sexually assaulting teenage girls in a previous decade.[1]

Many of us may disagree with Eugene Scott, or the secular media at large, but we can't ignore the ramifications these perceptions, right or wrong, have on our next generations. As Jesus-followers we may not care what *The Washington Post*, CNN, or Fox News has to say, but we had better never forget the forward momentum of the revolutionary kingdom will stop dead in its tracks if we lose the generations who must carry the mission of Christ forward.

It's already a struggle to reach them, regardless of how Christians and the church culturally present themselves. The Pew Research Center has reported more than a third of young adults are religiously unaffiliated. In fact, 36 percent of the youngest millennials, born between 1990 and 1996, are religious "nones" (they say they are atheists or agnostics, or their religion is "nothing in particular"). That's twice the percentage of my own age category.[2]

It's not just the "nones" that concern me, however. Young adults who were brought up within a faith community are also choosing to walk away. According to Barna, millennials who opt out of church do so for three primary reasons: the church's irrelevance, its hypocrisy, and moral failures within its leadership.[3]

Following the 2018 midterm election, *The New York Times* ran a fascinating profile piece featuring several interviews with young millennial evangelicals described as "questioning the typical ties between evangelicalism and Republican politics." Those interviewed for the article indicated the alignment between faith and politics in their experience had "caused schisms within their families. And many described a real struggle with an administration they see as hostile to immigrants, Muslims, L.G.B.T.Q. people, and the poor." One of the young adults interviewed shared, "I gave a communion message in 2016—it was, 'Our God chooses to die the death of all these marginalized people. He dies like Matthew Shepard, like a kid at the hand of the state. He was a refugee.' My church reprimanded me for 'abusing the pulpit.' Other members used it to openly stump for Trump and say hateful things about Muslims and L.G.B.T.

citizens." It's no wonder she finds herself disillusioned with the church of her childhood.[4]

My goal in this chapter is not to convince you which political party or candidate to support or which network news to watch. I believe many politicians are driven, deep down, by a desire, even if ill-informed or badly executed, to accomplish some good in the world. ABC, CBS, NBC, CNN, and Fox all offer good and bad points. Vote for whom you want; watch the news you want. But let's stop wrapping the Bible in an American flag, then further shrouding it with a political partisan framework. Our first loyalty is always to the Rebel Jesus and his mission. We have to be the people of God, not the people of one particular platform. I hate abortion, for example; I wish it didn't exist. But I can't defeat it by basing my moral compass on anything—or anyone—other than Jesus. We might be able to win a battle by aligning ourselves with a worldly force or system, but we will never win the war that way. I know. I cheated and jumped ahead to the final book in the Bible.

I encourage each of us to do some serious soul-searching on a daily basis. I like to use Isaiah 5:20 as my spiritual check when I start to become more passionate about my politics than my faith:

> Doom to those who call evil good and good evil,
> who present darkness as light and light as darkness,
> who make bitterness sweet and sweetness bitter.

I want to stop messing that up. It's so easy to put our news source in the place of honor that should be reserved for our life source.

A Kingdom of All Races

Before we can be a powerful, revolutionary force for defeating the "-isms" that divide, we first have to acknowledge our own culpability in perpetuating—or at least tolerating—them.

Each time we in the US celebrate a perceived win over the evils of racism, such as the Emancipation Proclamation, *Brown v. Board of Education*, the passage of the Civil Rights Act, or others, soon enough troubling events happen and trends emerge to remind us we have a long way to go.

In 2013, the controversial Black Lives Matter movement had its genesis as a hashtag after George Zimmerman was acquitted for killing seventeen-year-old Trayvon Martin the year before. The movement was further fueled in 2014, when two more African American men died—Michael Brown in Ferguson, Missouri, and Eric Garner in New York City—each through police action. Soon it seemed as if each new day's headline featured a black man dying a violent death, and new protests.

The plea of "Why can't we all just get along?" is perhaps better stated, "Why can't we all just begin to work on understanding each other?" Consider some statistics that show how differently blacks and whites in the US experience discrimination. In 2017, the Public Religion Research Institute (PRRI) indicated, not surprisingly, that nearly 90 percent of black Americans believe there is a great deal of current discrimination against blacks in America. Only 49 percent of white Americans agree. Forty-three percent of Republicans polled even felt whites are more likely to experience discrimination in the US than are blacks.[5]

The US Census has projected that by 2043, nonwhite races will form the majority of the US population. A PRRI poll revealed more than half of white evangelical Protestants view that impending shift in majority as a negative development.[6]

Why are so many of us who are white Christians fearful? What drives us to see ourselves as victims or losers in a zero-sum game instead of remembering we are part of the kingdom of God—a God of unlimited resources who is by, for, and about all God's people—regardless of color or political affiliation?

Robert P. Jones, who founded PRRI, published *The End of White Christian America* in 2017. He noted 80 percent of white evangelicals and 86 percent of white mainline Protestants have completely white social networks. How as a church will we ever defeat the evils of racism if we never sit down to dinner with someone who is a different color than us?[7] Jones also notes the number of white evangelicals is steadily declining while evangelicals of color are not sharing the same fate.

At this point, I can choose to be fearful about that shift, or I can choose to reach out and celebrate this new thing God is doing. I can connect with all my sisters and brothers, regardless of color, to be a community of light in a world God so loves. But I can't do that without first taking a position of humility, a position where I do more listening than speaking, more learning than teaching. And neither can you.

OK, so how do we do this in concrete ways?

First, Christians need to work harder to desegregate ourselves. Although diversity appears to be increasing in our churches, where Sunday morning has been described as the most segregated hour in America, we still have a long way to go. Eight in ten American churchgoers still worship at a site where a single ethnic or racial group makes up 80 percent of the congregation. We can't get to know each other better if we've never met in the first place.[8]

Ginghamsburg Church is a multisite congregation. I love all the campuses, but I have a special place in my heart for our Fort McKinley Campus, located in a socioeconomically challenged neighborhood in northwest Dayton. The Fort McKinley neighborhood is racially diverse, approximately half white and half African American. Being located in a diverse community, however, does not guarantee a diverse church.

Fort McKinley was a church before Ginghamsburg entered the picture. By the time the Fort became a Ginghamsburg Church community, it had dwindled to a congregation of approximately forty aging white folks. Although some had attended the church for sixty years or more, they no longer lived in the community. They had been part of the white flight to the suburbs years before.

The last thing I want to do is criticize those forty faithful followers. They wanted to reach their diverse community; they just weren't sure how. After the Fort McKinley faithful voted unanimously to become part of Ginghamsburg, the congregation demographics began to change almost immediately. The congregation reached outside its walls and transformed worship to be more contextual. The Fort remains one of the most diverse congregations I have ever attended or preached in. I love it.

However, if I'm honest, there have been challenges in cross-campus relationships between the Fort and our original, majority-white Tipp City Campus. White privilege, especially the inability of white folks like me to see it or admit we have it, is often at the core of those challenges. We can especially frustrate people when we walk into another community or context and act like we have it all figured out, or like we are there to help them learn and do what they are incapable of doing on their own. Let me give a few examples.

First of all, at Tipp City, which as the largest campus receives the most direct media team support, we had the habit, all well-intended, of putting together video pieces about the Fort that portrayed Fort McKinley more as our mission field than as a sister campus. The stories tended to be all about how our Tipp folks would go and serve at the Fort, not features about effective ministry the Fort was doing on its own. For instance, early on Sunday mornings Fort McKinley hosts a free breakfast worship called Soul Food Café that is frequented by homeless people and guests of area shelters. A number of Tipp City life groups and individuals have traveled to the Fort to serve as part of the breakfast volunteer team. That's a wonderful thing to do. But we started to hear complaints from our Fort staff: "Why can't you just come down some time and worship with us? Why do you serve breakfast and leave?" In other words, the staff was pointing out that ultimately the breakfast ministry is about being in and building relationships—not "doing good for poor folk."

Other misunderstandings can also arise. Typically, all Ginghamsburg campuses feature the same message series in the same season, although the messages themselves are contextualized. A few years ago, we did one of my all-time favorite February worship series, "Winter Blues." The worship center had a bit of a blues club feel, with café tables up front and around the worship space perimeter. Pretzels on the tables and a featured "blues" song each week added to the series' appeal. At the Tipp City Campus, our stage design team had a custom piece of art created to hang on the wall—it was in the shape of an oversized guitar with the words "Winter Blues" written on it with neon lights in the series' font. It was the perfect touch.

We did not create the same artwork for the Fort McKinley Campus. The windows in the Fort worship center did not allow for the same darkened room and stage that made the oversized guitar and neon "pop." And, economically and contextually, the piece made more sense in Tipp City. However, it was easy for a few people at other campuses to see the lack of the same opportunity in a different light. Why only Tipp City? Was the Fort congregation considered too poor to care about the finer things, or were middle-class whites seen as more deserving of privilege?

We have learned three things are key: *communication, communication, communication.* But the most crucial piece of all is figuring out how to be in authentic relationship with one another. As a white man, I need to enter into these relationships with humility, not hubris; with open hands, not a supercilious heart.

As Christians in general, we have some work to do. Often our congregations reflect our dinner tables. Who is at your table?

I am a Cincinnati native who attended a diverse high school in the 1960s. I became part of the Jesus Freak phenomenon as the Civil Rights Movement continued to unfold. Activism for better race relations was part of my college years. My wife, Carolyn, and I started a scholarship fund for students at my high school alma mater, and there is nothing I love more than hanging out with those really impressive kids. But, I have to confess that in most of my years at Ginghamsburg and our largely white Tipp City community, my own social network became far too monochrome in the direction of white. We have got to be intentional—multiethnic churches and communities will not happen by accident.

What we say and do as Christians also matters. When we fail to call out politicians, pundits, religious leaders, or celebrities that evince either blatant or subtle shades of racism, shame on us. Kingdom politics require us to be peacemakers, not peacekeepers. We are our brothers' and sisters' keepers.

One of the most troubling trends right now that I can't help but attribute in part to racism is the xenophobia that has focused all attention on the US-Mexico border. I don't think this question will win me any friends, but would we have the same fears and vehement desire to wall people out if those attempting to find refuge within our borders were white, English speaking, and Canadian?

We are making this issue a security crisis based on fear and driven by the desire to ensure our own comfort and safety, when from the kingdom-of-God's perspective it is a dire humanitarian crisis that flies in the face of Scripture's command to love your neighbor as yourself.

I could quote thousands of news stories at this point detailing exactly what I mean by humanitarian crisis. You have no doubt read many of them. Instead I want to share about a recent conversation with Kathleen (Katie) Kersh.

Katie is the daughter of one of our Ginghamsburg leadership board members and an immigration attorney and advocate. She is all too keenly aware of what is happening at the border, and especially in my home state of Ohio. She serves as a staff attorney for ABLE (Advocates for Basic Legal Equality), out of the Toledo-based nonprofit's Dayton location. She focuses on helping immigrants, particularly agricultural workers, with legal issues ranging from acquiring legal status to addressing worker exploitation and immigrant victimization. The immigrants Katie meets often face work exploitation and are all too frequently also the victims of crimes. Katie describes them as "most vulnerable of the vulnerable because of their undocumented status." They are fearful to report crimes to law enforcement, afraid their interaction with police could start a chain of events resulting in deportation.

I asked Katie what she sees as the biggest fallacies the American public believes about immigrants. In a matter of seconds, she rattled off three.

First, she mentioned the popular perception that immigrants are dangerous people putting American lives at risk. She could cite several sources indicating that this belief is simply untrue. Immigrants are far less likely to commit crime than native-born Americans. Immigrants have much more to lose if caught. Katie's clients are far more likely to have been victims of crimes than to have committed them.

The second "time-honored fallacy," as she called it, is the scarcity mentality mind-set that causes citizens to claim immigrants are stealing American jobs. In Ohio, Katie indicated immigrants work in industries typically considered undesirable by others because they are more dangerous or low-paying. "Most immigrants work in sectors that are actually endangered because not enough American workers want those jobs," she said. She named private home construction and the agriculture sector as prime examples. Katie pointed out that although mechanization plays a huge role in Ohio agriculture, many crops like berries and lettuce have to be harvested by hand.

The final fallacy that made her shake her head is the idea that "immigrants are a threat to my life, my language, my religion." Katie first pointed out the American "experience" we know today has been built out of other cultures' influences. The ports of San Francisco and Ellis Island alone made sure of that. Then she said, "On the other hand, people coming to the US want the 'American Dream' as Americans have defined it. They respect our educational system and rule of law. They want to be a part of it, not to challenge it."

Katie, who is a Christian, has been an attorney for six years. Katie said she always knew she wanted to be part of nonprofit work from an early age and applied to law school with the ultimate goal of providing legal assistance to people who are the most vulnerable. She has chosen a big job. When I asked her about what kept her up at nights, she named two things.

First, she worries about all the other needs the immigrant families have that ABLE is not positioned to meet. Even tasks many people find routine, like finding medical treatment or opening a checking account, can be formidable obstacles to immigrants.

Katie indicated she is also dismayed by what she sees as current legal violations in the treatment of immigrants, indicating the country is "not respecting the protections that we were founded upon." For instance, she pointed out that being in the US without legal status is not a crime—it's a civil violation of the Immigration and Nationality Act. She pointed out, "There is no jail time for civil violations, and yet we are detaining immigrants in criminal cells."

Katie then related the story of a woman we will call Marie, who first entered the US without permission in 2002. Marie was working at a meat-processing plant during an ICE (Immigration and Customs Enforcement) raid in 2007 that initiated deportation procedures. After her case was investigated, she was allowed to stay and continue the lengthy process to acquire legal status as long as she checked in regularly and maintained a clean record. Marie consistently complied. However, all the negativity and refocused attention on immigrants in 2017 led to ICE "grabbing her" again, as Katie described it. Marie was deported this time, despite being the mother of four children who were left in the US, and in the face of gang threats made against her and her family in the Mexican community to which she was forced to return. Her second seizure by ICE had happened in the middle of a day when her children were at home alone. Her fourth and youngest child requires observation and care because of a medical condition that provokes unpredictable seizures, and Marie was the only trained caregiver in the family.

Her Catholic church family in the US, where Marie was a valued parishioner, helped bring Marie's case to the attention of lawmakers and ABLE. The Sixth Circuit Court of Appeals eventually agreed to reopen the case, and Marie has now returned to her children. Immigration authorities wanted to detain her in jail as her case was considered, but she is currently out on bond.

Marie's children were traumatized by the separation, and its effects linger. Katie said, "What are the values of our country if we are not protecting children who are fleeing persecution?" She continued, "A few years ago I lost my sister who had young children. My heart broke for my niece and nephew. It was so hard because as much as I loved them, there was nothing that I or anyone could have done to protect them. In Marie's case, we can protect the children. Why would you ever separate a mom from her kids when you don't have to?"

I asked Katie for what she would say to churches and Jesus-followers on behalf of the immigrants, those whom God's word directs us not to mistreat or oppress (Exodus 22:21)—those whom we are directed to love (Deuteronomy 10:19). Katie said, "If you have church members who are immigrants, you need to rally around them. Show them the love and support that is too difficult for them to find elsewhere. ABLE can't meet all of the immigrant needs; there are too many requests. Educate yourself; be an advocate. Create an ecumenical network to partner together on meeting immigrant needs."

Katie concluded, "The Bible is incredibly clear about welcoming the stranger, judging not lest we be judged, and treating others as we want to be treated. We may be different from one another, but we are all children of the same God."

The apostle John once wrote, "But the person who hates a brother or sister is in the darkness and lives in the darkness, and doesn't know where to go because the darkness blinds the eyes" (1 John 2:11). Friends, it's well past time to take our self-focused blinders off and step boldly into the light and love of Christ.

A Gender-Inclusive Kingdom

Here are a few things I find completely astounding as I write this chapter:

- An Equal Rights Amendment to the US Constitution ensuring civil rights aren't denied on the basis of gender still hasn't passed.
- The world at large continues to make the very shortsighted decision to undervalue, underdeploy, and underinvest in the brain power, skills, and voices of roughly half of the world's population.
- One of the most gifted pastors and communicators I know still gets spiteful comments when she preaches from the pulpit.

Earlier this month, Rachel Billups, an ordained elder in The United Methodist Church, preached a strong message from the Ginghamsburg stage. This event was not in and of itself unusual. Rachel is Ginghamsburg's pastor at the Tipp City Campus and has been one of Ginghamsburg's primary preachers since 2014. The church communications team posted a picture of Rachel with a quote from her message on the church Facebook page.

Within hours, a nonattendee had jumped on the post, pointing out in no uncertain terms why he believed a woman pastor was completely inappropriate. Our team invited him to contact us for dialogue around his concern. Of course, that didn't happen. His second post appeared instead, starting with the words, "Since your church does not want to be a biblical church here you go," followed by the same verses from 1 Timothy that fearful people have always liked to quote when they believe that their privilege or primacy is in question. Really? Why do we continue to quote the same few verses, set within a very specific context, while completely ignoring the Junias, Phoebes, Priscillas, and Lydias of the New Testament? Jesus' mother Mary was herself no slacker, nor were the other strong women with whom Jesus surrounded himself.

The Old Testament, too, paints a picture of powerful female leadership. Miriam was one of the three leaders used by God to lead God's people out of slavery in Egypt (Micah 6:4). Deborah was arguably the most kick-butt prophet of them all, since God raised her up to be one of the judges who ruled the tribes of Israel before Saul became their king. Deborah was, in essence, the commander-in-chief, ensuring military success and the rule of justice that positioned the people of Israel to experience forty years of peace in a turbulent era.

The examples do not stop there. My best partners in ministry and mission have actually always been women, starting with my wife, Carolyn. Her faith and commitment to Jesus are unmatched. Carolyn is also a gifted discipler and remains one of the strongest communicators I know.

Tammy Kelley, originally a dental hygienist, started serving as Ginghamsburg's unpaid hospitality coordinator in the early 1990s and grew into an executive director role as the church grew. She later moved on to leadership at Willow Creek Community Church and Vanderbloemen, a church staffing executive search firm.

Kim Miller was my partner and the creative force behind multisensory worship and the media reformation.

Reverend Sue Nilson Kibbey blew discipleship and staff leadership practices out of the water during her tenure at Ginghamsburg.

My current writing and ministry partner in my firm Passionate Churches LLC is Karen Perry Smith.

I may have been the ass on which Jesus rode into the little burg of Ginghamsburg in 1979, but the miracles God has accomplished in that place would not have happened if these women and others had not also been called and gifted for such a time as this.

Why are we still having this conversation? It's crazy. If God has always seen fit to deploy women as coworkers and leaders within the revolutionary kingdom, why is it still a debated question within the church? Of course, the culture isn't doing any better than the church. Although the words "me too" were first used in 2006 by activist Tarana Burke, they really exploded into public consciousness when actress Alyssa Milano encouraged the use of #metoo as a Twitter hashtag as repeated allegations about Harvey Weinstein and other powerful men surfaced. Pay inequity, sexual objectification, sexual harassment and worse remain far too frequent experiences in the day-to-day lives of women.

Women face biases against them from the get-go that have never challenged me as a male. Whether you voted for or intensely dislike Hillary Clinton, you need to understand she had at least one difficult obstacle to surmount as a woman presidential candidate her opponent never had to face—the likeability issue. Likeability and success go hand-in-hand for men. The more powerful or successful you are, your likeability goes up. For women the opposite is true. The more successful or ambitious you are perceived to be, the more your likeability goes down.[9]

As the dad of a daughter and the proud papa of four granddaughters, I find all of this makes me crazy! My granddaughters should grow up in a world where they can run for office and be the smart, powerful, *and* likeable women they are quickly becoming. In the next presidential election, I want to cast my vote on the basis of candidate competency, whether male or female, not based on some wrongheaded gender bias.

From the beginning, we read in Scripture,

> *God created humankind in his image,*
> *in the image of God he created them;*
> *male and female he created them.*
> *(Genesis 1:27, NRSV)*

And in the final days, God says,

> *I will pour out my Spirit upon everyone;*
> *your sons and your daughters will prophesy. . . .*
> *I will also pour out my*
> *spirit on the male and female slaves.*
> *(Joel 2:28-29)*

Clearly, God doesn't eliminate the gifts, graces, and voices of half of creation in God's revolutionary kingdom. Why do we?

THE DIVIDING WALLS OF HOSTILITY

Sadly, devaluing God's people doesn't stop with racism and sexism.

Within The United Methodist Church, my tribe for nearly fifty years, the divisiveness surrounding homosexuality is threatening to tear apart the denomination. How do you divide up the church of the revolutionary kingdom?

Ginghamsburg Church has always followed UMC polity regarding homosexuality. At the same time, it has become a safe place without hate for many LGBTQ people, including married couples with children. Yet Ginghamsburg's largest campus is also in the heart of one of the most conservative political counties in Ohio. Through word and action, we do the best we can to continue to emphasize, "Jesus is the issue. Everything else is simply a conversation." Throughout my ministry at Ginghamsburg, even before full inclusion of LGBTQ sisters and brothers became the most hotly debated topic within United Methodism and other congregations, I preached and tried my best to practice love and grace. I need God to figure it all out on the back end. Our job is to love, not to judge.

A few years ago, Carolyn and I issued an open invitation to the LGBTQ folks within the congregation to join us in our home as a safe space for open conversation. It was a night of healing and love. I want that for all of God's people. If I am wrong in my determination to love without judgment, I expect God someday to give me a slap on the wrist. At that point I will deserve it. But I do not want to stand in front of God as the sheep are separated from the goats if my actions have ever kept anyone from experiencing the love of God that is found in Christ Jesus (Romans 8:38-39). Now *that's* a serious offense.

Within the culture and the church we are also struggling with ageism. Recently, a close friend of mine who pioneered the Ginghamsburg movement with me shared his pain at realizing he was in his early seventies. He feared the best of everything was in his past. I reminded him that seventy was young for biblical heroes. For one, Moses was an octogenarian when he confronted the powerful pharaoh and led God's people out of Egyptian bondage.

As I look across Ginghamsburg Church, I see many vibrant grandparents still leading the charge on our social ministries. The seasoned saints are incredibly essential. Yet, without the engagement and commitment of the next generations, the church will cease to exist.

Last year, an article in *Forbes* titled "Boomers Are Sociopaths, Millennials Are Bums: Rethinking the Generation Blame Game" caught my eye. The author, Joseph Coughlin, described the unhelpful, broad characterizations boomers and millennials seem to be making about each other, at least according to the media, and indicated the dangers of using "shorthand and sloppy thinking" to describe whole age ranges. As Coughlin noted, "Like the Boomers before them, the Millennials are also being overly simplified into one monolithic storyline." Given there is a fifteen-year age difference between the youngest and oldest ages embodied in the "millennial" designation, of course they don't all think, act, or vote alike. I almost laughed out loud when Coughlin made this point, "Donald Trump is a Baby Boomer; so is Judith Butler; so is Jimmy Buffett; so is Barack Obama. If someone can figure out what those four all have in common, I will be glad to hear it. Who of them, exactly, *screwed us over?*"[10]

Two to three times each week, I find a new headline in my news feed that lists yet one more product or industry millennials are allegedly destroying or putting out of business. The tension between the two generations has become common news-feed fodder and a frequent focus of office water cooler conversations. As if we don't have enough "enemies" to worry about already, we have to start competing with our grandparents—or our grandchildren.

God's revolutionary kingdom is not only to be multigenerational, all generations together, it is to be intergenerational, all generations interacting together for the common good of God's movement. What's the difference? A multigenerational church may have all ages represented, but the mission and ministry are too often segregated by age demographic in a "never the two shall meet" scenario. There are few opportunities for one generation to be empowered and made better by another—whether it's old saints mentoring the young or young voices influencing and informing the seasoned for the sake of the revolutionary kingdom.

The New Testament church had its own struggles in this area, leading the apostle Paul to counsel his apprentice in ministry, Timothy, to let no one despise him for his youth and instead diligently be an example to all generations (1 Timothy 4:12). Peter likewise reminded his readers, "In the same way, I urge you who are younger: accept the authority of the elders. And everyone, clothe yourselves with humility toward each other" (1 Peter 5:5). *Everyone* in biblical Greek still means "everyone."

For He Himself Is Our Peace

When did we replace our kingdom-of-God worldview with a corrupted and corrupting cultural or political worldview that treats diversity as a threat? What are we afraid of?

The diversity of all creation, especially people, is one of our creative God's very best gifts. As disciples of the Rebel Jesus, our worldview and our actions must return to reflecting his—an unswerving commitment to intentional and inclusive diversity, justice for all, and amazing grace. In times of turmoil, conflict, or uncertainty—and that certainly describes the twenty-first century—citizens of the revolutionary kingdom must choose intentionally and consistently to err on the side of God's grace, first for ourselves and then for *everyone else.*

It's what Kingdom people do.

Acknowledgments

I want to express a deep debt of gratitude to the Abingdon Press team who helped make the vision for this work a present reality, especially editor Maria Mayo and Susan Salley, who has been my publisher for more than twelve years.

Karen Perry Smith has served as my book-writing partner and researcher since 2012 and helped significantly in crafting the mission and message of this book.

I am very thankful to the following dynamic pastors within my United Methodist tribe for their time and wisdom in shaping the video study that accompanies this text: Jacob Armstrong, Rachel Billups, Matt Miofsky, and Lisa Yebuah.

My wife, Carolyn, is always my biggest cheerleader and accountability partner for all things I commit to for serving Jesus.

Finally, I would be remiss if I failed to mention two spiritual giants who helped shape my understanding of the revolutionary kingdom of God since my early days of ministry, Howard Snyder and Will Willimon, as well as the saints that have gone before us, St. Francis of Assisi, St. Clare of the Poor, and Dietrich Bonhoeffer.

Notes

Chapter 1: The Gospel of the Kingdom of God

1   Mike Slaughter, *Renegade Gospel: The Rebel Jesus* (Nashville: Abingdon Press, 2014), 43-44.

2   Joe Heim, "Jerry Falwell Jr. Can't Imagine Trump 'Doing Anything That's Not Good for the Country,'" *The Washington Post*, January 1, 2019, https://www.washingtonpost.com/lifestyle/magazine/jerry -falwell-jr-cant-imagine-trump-doing-anything-thats-not-good-for -the-country/2018/12/21/6affc4c4-f19e-11e8-80d0-f7e1948d55f4 _story.html?utm_term=.9747f2d2a406, accessed April 15, 2019.

3   N. T. Wright, *Surprised by Hope* (New York: HarperOne, 2008), 214-215.

4   Louis Evely, *In the Christian Spirit*, as quoted, with permission from the author, in Rueben P. Job and Norman Shawchuck, *A Guide to Prayer for Ministers and Other Servants* (Nashville: The Upper Room, 1983), 336.

5   David Brooks, "How We Are Ruining America," *The New York Times*, July 11, 2017, https://www.nytimes.com/2017/07/11/opinion /how-we-are-ruining-america.html, accessed April 15, 2019.

6   Ben Zipperer, "The Erosion of the Federal Minimum Wage Has Increased Poverty, Especially for Black and Hispanic Families," *Economic Policy Institute*, June 13, 2018, https://www.epi.org /publication/the-erosion-of-the-federal-minimum-wage-has -increased-poverty-especially-for-black-and-hispanic-families, accessed April 15, 2019.

7 Quoted by Leo J. O'Donovan, "The Vocation of a Theologian," *America: The Jesuit Review*, November 28, 2005, https://www.americamagazine.org/issue/552/faith-focus/vocation-theologian, accessed March 28, 2019.

8 Robert Ellsberg, *Blessed Among Us: Day by Day with Saintly Witnesses* (Collegeville, MN: Liturgical Press, 2016), 621.

9 Rebecca Van Noord, "Albert Mohler: Equipping the Church for the Mission" (on Christian Engagement in Politics and Culture), Bible Study Magazine.com, http://www.biblestudymagazine.com/al-mohler, accessed April 15, 2019.

10 "Oscar Romero," Wikipedia, https://en.wikipedia.org/wiki/%C3%93scar_Romero, accessed May 5, 2019.

11 Oscar Romero, *The Scandal of Redemption: When God Liberates the Poor, Saves Sinners, and Heals Nations* (Walden, NY: Plough Publishing House, 2018), 55.

12 Oscar Romero, *The Scandal of Redemption*, 55.

13 "Syrian Refugee Crisis: Facts, FAQs, and How to Help," World Vision, https://www.worldvision.org/refugees-news-stories/syrian-refugee-crisis-facts, accessed April 15, 2019.

14 Mike Jordan Laskey, "American Flags Don't Belong in Church Sanctuaries," *National Catholic Reporter*, September 28, 2017, https://www.ncronline.org/news/opinion/young-voices/american-flags-dont-belong-church-sanctuaries, accessed April 15, 2019.

Chapter 2: The Counterculture Kingdom Community

1 "Our Mission Statement," *Joshua Recovery Ministries*, http://www.joshualife.org/index.php/about/our-mission-statement, accessed April 15, 2019.

2 "Americans Divided on the Importance of Church," Barna: FRAMES, March 24, 2014, https://www.barna.com/research/americans-divided-on-the-importance-of-church/#.V-hxhLVy6FD, accessed April 15, 2019; as summarized by Sam Eaton, "12 Reasons Millennials are OVER Church," Recklessly Alive, September 29, 2016, https://www.recklesslyalive.com/12-reasons-millennials-are-over-church/, accessed April 15, 2019.

3   Ed Stetzer, quoted by Audrey Barrick, "How Do Unchurched Americans View Christianity?," *The Christian Post*, January 9, 2008, https://www.christianpost.com/news/how-do-unchurched -americans-view-christianity.html, accessed April 15, 2019.

4   Mike Slaughter, "Fighting Evil—Like Jiu Jitsu," *United Methodist Insight*, June 16, 2016, http://um-insight.net/in-the-church /practicing-faith/fighting-evil-%E2%80%93-like-jiu-jitsu/, accessed April 15, 2019.

5   *Give Us This Day: Daily Prayer for Today's Catholic*, June 14, 2016, https://giveusthisday.org, accessed April 15, 2019.

6   *Give Us This Day: Daily Prayer for Today's Catholic*, March 24, 2018, 263, https://giveusthisday.org, accessed April 15, 2019.

7   John Wesley, Sermon 36, "The Law Established through Faith, II," *Works of Wesley* (Bicentennial 2:38); quoted by David N. Field, "Embodying the Love of God: A Wesleyan Vision for the Church and the One Church Model Part 1: The Church and the Missio Dei," Grace in the Fractures, August 22, 2018, https://davidnfield .wordpress.com/2018/08/22/embodying-the-love-of-god-a-wesleyan -vision-for-the-church-and-the-one-church-model-part-1-the -church-and-the-missio-dei/#_edn6, accessed April 15, 2019.

Chapter 3: Revolutionary Authority

1   John Wesley, Sermon #12 "The Witness of Our Own Spirit," quoted in Mike Slaughter, *Spiritual Entrepreneurs: 6 Principles for Risking Renewal* (Nashville: Abingdon Press, 1994, 1995), 48.

2   John Wesley, *The Works of the Reverend John Wesley*, Journal, June 5, 1766; quoted in Mike Slaughter, *Spiritual Entrepreneurs: 6 Principles for Risking Renewal* (Nashville: Abingdon Press, 1994, 1995), 49.

3   Quoted in Robert Ellsberg, *Blessed Among Us: Day by Day with Saintly Witnesses* (Collegeville, MN: The Liturgical Press, 2016), 147, https://books.google.com/books?id=osC5DAAAQBAJ&pg =PA147&lpg=PA147&dq=%22Very+soon+the+Bible+won %E2%80%99t+be+allowed+to+cross+our+borders %22&source=bl&ots=o93_v-ZMzk&sig =ACfU3U34TOK7w6QEoAlAm6VtUKmIRokk2w&hl=en&sa =X&ved=2ahUKEwimpLOqw9PhAhXsYt8KHQtCCDEQ6AEwA- HoECAYQAQ#v=onepage&q=%22Very%20soon%20the

%20Bible%20won%E2%80%99t%20be%20allowed%20to%20
cross%20our%20borders%22&f=false, accessed April 15, 2019.

4   For references to the two General Conferences, see "Biblical
    Authority," *The GC2019 Delegate*, December 2018, Issue 2,
    https://mainstreamumc.com/wp-content/uploads/2018/12/2018
    -12-17theDelegate.pdf, accessed May 6, 2019.

5   Philip Pullela, "Slain Salvadoran Bishop Romero and Pope Paul VI
    Become Saints," Reuters, October 14, 2018, https://www.reuters.com
    /article/us-pope-saints/slain-salvadoran-bishop-romero-and-pope
    -paul-vi-become-saints-idUSKCN1MO098, accessed April 15, 2019.

6   A. G. Dickens, *The Counter Reformation* (Great Britain: Harcourt,
    Brace & World, 1969), 37.

7   Richard Rohr, "Jesus: Modeling an Evolving Faith: Patience," Center
    for Action and Contemplation (Albuquerque, NM), January 4, 2019,
    https://cac.org/patience-2019-01-04/, accessed May 7, 2019.

8   William G. McLoughlin, "Revivalism," *The Rise of Adventism:
    Religion and Society in Mid-Nineteenth-Century America*, ed. Edwin
    Scott Gaustad (New York: Harper & Row, 1974), 132.

9   Dorothy Day, *From Union Square to Rome*, 1938, https://www
    .catholicworker.org/dorothyday/articles/204.html,
    accessed April 15, 2019.

10 Dorothy Day, "Love Is the Measure," *The Catholic Worker Movement*,
    June 1946, https://www.catholicworker.org/dorothyday/articles/425
    .html, accessed May 7, 2019.

11 Tony Perrottet, "Ancient Greek Temples of Sex," *The Smart Set*
    (Philadelphia, PA: Drexel University Pennoni Honors College),
    November 21, 2007, https://thesmartset.com/article11210701/,
    accessed April 15, 2019.

Chapter 4: Kingdom Politics

1   Anna Papadopoulos, "Ranked: The Most Powerful People in the
    World, 2018," *CEOWorld Magazine*, October 23, 2018, https://
    ceoworld.biz/2018/10/23/most-powerful-people-in-the-world
    -2018/, accessed April 15, 2019.

2   "Forbes Releases 2018 List of the World's Most Powerful People,"
    Forbes.com, May 8, 2018, https://www.forbes.com/sites

/forbespr/2018/05/08/forbes-releases-2018-list-of-the-worlds-most
-powerful-people/#4d700b48719c, accessed April 15, 2019.

3   Sue Scheff, "The Impact of Public Shaming in a Digital World,"
Psychology Today, July 5, 2018, https://www.psychologytoday.com
/us/blog/shame-nation/201807/the-impact-public-shaming-in
-digital-world, accessed April 15, 2019.

4   "Suicide Rates Rising Across the U.S.," Centers for Disease
Control and Prevention, June 7, 2018, https://www.cdc.gov/media
/releases/2018/p0607-suicide-prevention.html, accessed April 15,
2019.

5   *Give Us This Day: Daily Prayer for Today's Catholic*, 2018, 119,
https://giveusthisday.org, accessed April 15, 2019.

6   E. Stanley Jones, *The Christ of the Mount: A Working Philosophy of
Life* (New York: Abingdon Press, 1931), 81, https://archive.org
/stream/christofthemount009329mbp/christofthemount009329mbp
_djvu.txt, accessed April 15, 2019.

Chapter 5: Kingdom Economy

1   "Economy," Investopedia.com, April 1, 2018, https://www
.investopedia.com/terms/e/economy.asp, accessed April 15, 2019.

2   "Win-lose strategy," *Dictionary of International Trade*,
Globalnegotiator.com, https://www.globalnegotiator.com
/international-trade/dictionary/win-lose-strategy/, accessed
April 15, 2019.

3   Hunter Schwarz, "Millennials Are Much More Open to Socialism,"
CNN.com, June 28, 2018, https://www.cnn.com/2018/06/28/politics
/democratic-socialism-millennial-politics/index.html, accessed
April 15, 2019.

4   Mike Slaughter with Karen Perry Smith, *The Christian Wallet:
Spending, Giving, and Living with a Conscience* (Louisville:
Westminster John Knox Press, 2016), 15.

5   Biwa Kwan, "The Ten Most Costly Climate Change Disasters of
2018," SBS News, December 27, 2018, https://www.sbs.com.au/news
/the-ten-most-costly-climate-change-disasters-of-2018, accessed
April 15, 2019.

6   Intergovernmental Panel on Climate Change, *Global Warming of 1.5 °C*, https://www.ipcc.ch/sr15/, accessed April 15, 2019.

7   US Global Change Research Program, *Fourth National Climate Assessment, Volume II: Impacts, Risks, and Adaptation in the United States*, https://nca2018.globalchange.gov/, accessed April 15, 2019.

8   John Viljoen, "Cape Town Drought Highlights Water Scarcity Risk to Vulnerable Cities Globally: UBS," August 28, 2018, https://www.insurancejournal.com/news/international/2018/08/28/499303.htm, accessed April 15, 2019.

9   Jeff McMahon, "9 Things You Can Do About Climate Change," Forbes.com, January 23, 2017, https://www.forbes.com/sites/jeffmcmahon/2017/01/23/nine-things-you-can-do-about-climate-change/#c9ffdd680c7c, accessed April 15, 2019.

10 Maia Szalavitz, "Why Do We Think Poor People Are Poor Because of Their Own Bad Choices?," *The Guardian*, July 5, 2017, https://www.theguardian.com/us-news/2017/jul/05/us-inequality-poor-people-bad-choices-wealthy-bias, accessed April 15, 2019.

11 Steven Brill, "How Baby Boomers Broke America," *Time*, May 17, 2018, http://time.com/magazine/us/5280431/may-28th-2018-vol-191-no-20-u-s/, accessed April 15, 2019.

12 Robert Frank, "Richest 1% Now Owns Half the World's Wealth," *USA Today*, November 14, 2017, https://www.usatoday.com/story/money/2017/11/14/richest-1-now-owns-half-worlds-wealth/862916001/, accessed April 15, 2019.

13 Carmen Reinicke, "US Income Inequality Continues to Grow," CNBC.com, July 19, 2018, https://www.cnbc.com/2018/07/19/income-inequality-continues-to-grow-in-the-united-states.html, accessed April 15, 2019.

14 Daniel Kurt, "Are You in the Top One Percent of the World?," Investopedia.com, February 8, 2019, https://www.investopedia.com/articles/personal-finance/050615/are-you-top-one-percent-world.asp, accessed April 15, 2019.

15 Christopher Ingraham, "How Rising Inequality Hurts Everyone, Even the Rich," *The Washington Post*, February 6, 2018, https://www.washingtonpost.com/news/wonk/wp/2018/02/06/how-rising-inequality-hurts-everyone-even-the-rich/?noredirect=on&utm_term=.5e1bd8e438f7, accessed April 15, 2019.

Chapter 6: The "All In"

1   Eugene Scott, "Evangelicals Continue to Apply Moral Relativism in Dealing with Trump, But at What Cost?," *The Washington Post*, January 21, 2018, https://www.washingtonpost.com/news/the-fix /wp/2018/01/21/evangelicals-continue-to-apply-moral-relativism -in-dealing-with-trump-but-at-what-cost/?utm_term=. aeb437a8fba7, accessed April 15, 2019.

2   Michael Lipka, "Millennials Increasingly Are Driving Growth of 'Nones,'" Pew Research Center, May 12, 2015, https://www .pewresearch.org/fact-tank/2015/05/12/millennials-increasingly -are-driving-growth-of-nones/, accessed April 15, 2019.

3   "What Millennials Want When They Visit Church," Barna Group, March 4, 2015, https://www.barna.com/research/what-millennials -want-when-they-visit-church/, accessed April 15, 2019.

4   Elizabeth Dias, "'God Is Going to Have to Forgive Me': Young Evangelicals Speak Out," *The New York Times*, November 1, 2018, https://www.nytimes.com/2018/11/01/us/young-evangelicals -politics-midterms.html, accessed April 15, 2019.

5   Robert P. Jones, "Republicans More Likely to Say White Americans— Rather Than Black Americans—Face Discrimination," PRRI (Public Religion Research Institute), August 2, 2017, https://www.prri.org /spotlight/republicans-white-black-reverse-discrimination/, accessed April 15, 2019.

6   Alex Vandermaas-Peeler et al., "American Democracy in Crisis: The Challenges of Voter Knowledge, Participation, and Polarization," PRRI (Public Religion Research Institute), July 17, 2018, https:// www.prri.org/research/american-democracy-in-crisis-voters -midterms-trump-election-2018/, accessed April 15, 2019.

7   Daniel José Camacho, "How the Changing Church Will Define the Future of U.S. Politics," *Sojourners*, July 31, 2017, https://sojo.net /articles/how-changing-church-will-define-future-us-politics, accessed April 15, 2019.

8   Michael Lipka, "Many U.S. Congregations Are Still Racially Segregated, But Things Are Changing," Pew Research Center, December 8, 2014, https://www.pewresearch.org/fact -tank/2014/12/08/many-u-s-congregations-are-still-racially -segregated-but-things-are-changing-2/, accessed April 15, 2019.

9   Maria Katsarou, "Women & the Leadership Labyrinth: Howard vs Heidi," Leadership Psychology Institute, https://www .leadershippsychologyinstitute.com/women-the-leadership -labyrinth-howard-vs-heidi/, accessed April 15, 2019.

10   Joseph Coughlin, "Boomers Are Sociopaths, Millennials Are Bums: Rethinking the Generation Blame Game," Forbes.com, June 28, 2018, https://www.forbes.com/sites/josephcoughlin/2018/06/28 /boomers-are-sociopaths-millennials-are-bums-rethinking-the -generation-blame-game/#22e4f3d941e7, accessed April 15, 2019.